BACK TO THE BLACK

smart **investing**
@ your library®

A partnership between American Library Association
and FINRA Investor Education Foundation

ALA American Library Association

FINra Investor Education FOUNDATION

FINRA is proud to support the American Library Association

MICHAEL J MACMAHON

BACK TO THE
BLACK

HOW TO BECOME DEBT-FREE AND STAY THAT WAY

SilverWood

Published in 2015 by SilverWood Books
Second Edition

SilverWood Books Ltd
30 Queen Charlotte Street, Bristol, BS1 4HJ
www.silverwoodbooks.co.uk

The content of this book does not constitute specific financial advice.
The reader should thus take qualified advice before making any
important financial decisions. Every effort has been taken to ensure
that the information contained is accurate but neither the author nor
the publisher can take responsibility for any errors, inaccuracies or
omissions. References to organisations have been given for the purpose
of information and do not constitute a recommendation.

ISBN 978-1-78132-333-5 (paperback)
ISBN 978-1-78132-334-2 (ebook)

British Library Cataloguing in Publication Data
A CIP catalogue record for this book is available from
the British Library

Set in Myriad Pro by SilverWood Books
Printed on responsibly sourced paper

To my daughters, Caroline and Madeleine,
in the hope that they will never need it

Contents

Acknowledgements

During the planning and writing of this book I've had masses of practical support and advice from many friends and professional associates, who are listed below. Their support is much appreciated.

All the professionals listed provided their advice on a pro bono basis.

In alphabetical order, with apologies to anyone I may have overlooked: Tim Arnold (Tarrystone Consultants, Maidenhead); Erle Bryn (Con Motoh Consulting, Oslo); Gina Butler and Lynne Teague (Citizens Advice, Forest of Dean); Amba Chawla; Adrian Clay; Sean Emmett and D J Exell (Bishop Fleming & Co, Bristol); Melanie Giles (PJG Recovery, formerly Jones Giles Limited, Cardiff); Dan Holloway; Jenny Layton; Sean McManus; David Moody; Ali Reynolds; Steve Roberts; Barry Steel; Andy Steward (Citizens Advice, Bristol); John Steward (Steward & Co, London); Rachael Stock Anderson (Pearson Education); Nick Thomas (The Thomas Consultancy, Stratford upon Avon); Martin Tucker; Ann Waller (Ottakar's Bookstore – now Waterstone's – Gloucester); Len Warwick, RIP. (Warwick Butchart Associates, Cheltenham)

I acknowledge, moreover, the input of many public-, private- and voluntary-sector organisations working in this field, whose published information has been invaluable.

Thanks in particular to the following organisations for providing pro-bono advice and/or resources for this book:

- Citizens Advice Bureau, Bristol: for case studies.
- PJG Recovery (formerly Jones Giles Ltd): for Chapter 9 and "How to Find an Insolvency Practitioner."

Thanks also go to this edition's beta-readers Pete Dalby, Jenny Hammerton and Lisa Middle.

Special thanks to insolvency practitioner Melanie Giles for her vetting of Chapter 9 of this book; and for her expert, impartial advice at my time of crisis.

The case studies used in this book are based on actual situations. However the names of the people concerned have all been either changed or removed.

Foreword

Debt is a serious issue. I've spent enough of my life in debt to know how distressing and destabilising it can be. And it's not just caused by overspending, but can be the result of a tragedy, illness, or other traumatic event.

People who get into debt consequently often feel helpless. And if they're paying huge interest charges on the money they owe, they could well be heading for a financial disaster where their debts spiral totally out of control.

In short, being in problem debt is not a pleasant situation. Having experienced it personally I avoid borrowing money if at all possible. Sure, I have a mortgage, but that's planned debt. I know I can afford the repayments and have a set programme – including monthly overpayments – to clear the outstanding debt as soon as possible.

I write almost every week in *The Independent* about people who've got into financial difficulties for a number of different reasons. There was Sue who was diagnosed with cancer, lost her job because she had to take off so much time for treatment, and ended up almost homeless, before a debt charity stepped in to help her get back on her feet.

There was Dan, a well-paid banker who lived life to the full until he was suddenly made redundant and ended up losing everything because he couldn't pay off his debt. He eventually retrained and now works as a carpenter, a lot less well-off, but a lot wiser.

Michael MacMahon has been through the debt cycle, too, as you'll discover as you read his story. I know he never wants to repeat his experiences, but sharing them with others is a hugely helpful thing to do. One of the biggest hurdles to overcome when dealing with debt is admitting there's a problem, not just to family and friends, but to yourself.

Reading Michael's story of his descent into debt hell should help you realise that it's all too easy and not something you should necessarily blame yourself for. The difficult part, of course, is getting on top of the problem and climbing out of debt. But, again, Michael's story is a great eye-opener into just how that can be achieved and his constant advice throughout this book should prove pretty useful if you're in a similar situation.

To be honest, I'm not a fan of self-help books. They tend to be written by professional self-proclaimed 'gurus' who pull together a collection of over-used glib phrases and a smattering of common sense to sell tens of thousands of books that are probably not much good to anyone, apart from lining the pockets of the author.

Michael's book is precisely the opposite. It's written from the heart by a man who has been there. If you think you're the only person who's struggling to cope with debt, he'll show you that you're not and help you find ways to put your problems behind you. But only if you want to, of course. Getting out of debt is not easy. It will take self-discipline and sacrifice. If you're ready for that challenge then read on – and I wish you the greatest success.

SIMON READ, PERSONAL FINANCE EDITOR OF *THE INDEPENDENT* NEWSPAPER

Introduction

Why have I written this book? Put simply: a few years ago I went through a severe debt crisis. I survived it; and now I want to share what I learned from that painful experience.

I had started a business, which did well for several years and then began to lose money. For some time I turned a blind eye to the problem. By the time I started to face facts, I was very close to bankruptcy. However, with the help and support of friends and of a few professionals (one of whom happened also to be a good friend) I eventually avoided bankruptcy and came through the experience without permanent scars to my spirit and credit rating.

[That's not your story? You haven't got a business? It doesn't matter, I venture to suggest. By the end of this book I hope you will agree with me that however the situation arose – see Chapter 1, 'Causes of Debt' – the options for getting out of debt are basically the same.]

After I had managed to clear my debts and get 'back to the black', I decided to write a book from the perspective of someone who has been there, had the problem and found a way through it.

I want to share what I learned from my experiences. If what I've written helps you to get out of debt, this book will have served its purpose.

Back to the Black – How to become debt-free and stay that way is primarily aimed at people going through what I went through. If you have debts that have reached, or might soon reach, problem proportions – whether those debts are personal, business, or a combination of both – then this book is for you.

You'll read my story: where I went wrong; how and where I found unbiased advice and support; and how I found the solutions that eventually got me out of debt.

Most importantly, though, you'll learn what I hope you'll find to be a logical and step-by-step process to decide the best option in *your* situation.

You'll find chapters on the stress caused by debt and how to deal with it; on how to formulate your debt management goals; on how best to evaluate your current situation; and on how to develop a list of options for how to get from where you are now to where you want to be. Then I suggest how you might decide which option is best in your situation, how to formulate a plan, and how to communicate with your creditors while you put that plan into practice.

The context

I live in the UK. And as I've said, my own debt crisis happened when my business failed. Those are two aspects of my situation (my location; and the cause) that might well be totally different from your situation. It doesn't matter: I believe that no matter *where* in the world you live, and no matter what was the *cause* of your debt problem, the options open to you are basically the same.

My Story

Are you losing sleep over your debt situation? If so, you might be interested to read my story, because a few years ago I was in the same position. At the time I could see no way out of my problem; but with support (and free advice, of which there is lots available) I eventually found there were solutions.

The cause

In the late 1990s I had a debt crisis. It happened because I had a small business. It had been going well; but then work started to dry up.

At that time, credit was very easy to obtain. I had a couple of loans from banks and several credit cards; and those provided the working capital I needed to keep the business going. The debts built up; but I was convinced I could turn things around.

The crisis

By the time I finally realised that I couldn't turn it around, the problem was very severe. I owed money to 26 different creditors.

I could not envisage being able to get the debts down to a manageable level in less than five years. My creditors – mostly banks and credit card providers – would not give me that kind of time. Understandably.

My then accountant recommended bankruptcy. He even said there could never be a better time for me to go bankrupt. After a few years I would have been 'discharged' and debt-free. Yes, I would have had a rock-bottom credit rating, but maybe that was a price worth paying.

But there were, of course, other disadvantages to the bankruptcy route. Firstly, I had some occupational pensions, of the 'money purchase' type. They were not massive but they had been accumulated over a 30-year period. If I had become bankrupt, those pensions might well have been vulnerable.

Secondly, although I did not want to get into consumer debt again, I could foresee a time when I might want to get back on to the property ladder (that's a ladder I had well and truly fallen off by this time; the bruises lasted a while) and I knew that would be much more difficult if I were a discharged bankrupt.

Finally, the psychological aspect. We all have our attitudes to this; and whether you want to file for bankruptcy as a way out of the situation will depend partly on the size of your debts and partly on your psychological reaction to the prospect of being bankrupt. For me, bankruptcy was out.

[However, since the turn of the millennium in the UK it has become in many ways a more acceptable option, as both the stigma and the practical disadvantages have lessened greatly.]

In the UK we have a variation on bankruptcy, known as an IVA – an Individual Voluntary Arrangement (i.e. with your creditors). It's sometimes called 'bankruptcy lite' and it has many of the practical disadvantages of bankruptcy, though it does not have the same perceived stigma.

I talk about both bankruptcy and IVAs in Chapter 9.

The solution

In the end, I didn't file for bankruptcy. I didn't go for an IVA either, mostly because of what I was told by an old friend from my twenties; let's call him John. His view was that an IVA was in some ways worse than bankruptcy, though without the same stigma. As he said, "you'll have someone looking over your shoulder, and your bank accounts, for years".

I decided John was right and I should not go either for bankruptcy or an IVA, because a third and better solution was suggested by a very helpful insolvency practitioner.

Yes, she thought an IVA would work and her firm could arrange and manage it; but there were significant fees to be charged. She said there was an alternative solution. Did I think I could manage the process myself and make an offer for partial payment? If so, then I could self-administer my exit from debt.

I decided to adopt this approach. It's what I call in this book 'Plan C – Negotiate a Deal' and you'll find it in Chapter 10. I would deal with my creditors myself, rather than through an insolvency practitioner. This would get me to where I wanted to be – debt-free – while ensuring that my creditors got an acceptable amount.

So I went for Plan C and made an offer for full and final settlement. Eventually all my creditors, (apart from the Revenue, i.e. the income tax people, who never negotiate) agreed to the deal, though not before considerable correspondence. In the process my local branch of the UK's Citizens Advice organisation was of massive help.

I was also very lucky in that one of my very oldest friends is an accountant; let's call him Andrew. He did my tax return free of charge for several years, though I had never previously asked him to do any work for me, because I used to think one shouldn't mix friendship and business. However, once I had come clean and told him the mess I was in, Andrew put his solid shoulder to the proverbial wheel.

One of the most valuable things he did was to decimate my tax liability for previous years, by identifying tax losses and allowances that I could legitimately claim but had not claimed. That alone was a massive help; the Revenue (Her Majesty's Revenue & Customs, to give it its full name; our equivalent to the IRS in the USA) was one of my biggest creditors, and they very rarely negotiate away a penny of tax owed to them. Their debt is a 'primary charge' on your estate, thus if your case ever does go to a bankruptcy, they will get first bite at any funds available.

The moral here, apart from the necessity of having good friends, is the importance of being open with the people you are close to. That's something that I had not done; I felt considerable shame about my financial situation and had thus hidden it from my friends.

The whole point of my story is this. At the time, I thought my debt problem was insurmountable. It was certainly a very stressful time. However, with the help of some great advice and support, I came through the experience and I learned many things that were of great value. Now, with the benefit of hindsight (which, of course, always gives you 20:20 vision) I realise that it was only money. There are more important things in life.

There are many reasons why we get into debt, as you will read in this book. These problems often result from a combination of circumstances, rather than one single cause. I repeat my contention that whatever caused you to get into debt, the principles for getting out of the problem are the same. No apologies for that repetition.

I was not, and am not, happy with the fact that I was unable to pay my debts in full. After the event, however, I decided to write up what had happened, partly for my own benefit. I even thought that maybe it would make a couple of newspaper articles. If other people with debt problems could benefit from reading about my mistakes and what I'd learned, then something good would have come out of it all. Those articles eventually grew into this book.

In summary, my book is grounded in painful experience. I hope that you can benefit from reading about that experience. If you have debts, however they were caused, the principles for dealing with them are the same. The experiences you are going through are, of course, unique to your situation; but they may well have a lot in common with mine.

An update – January 2015

My story happened, as I said, in the late 1990s. You might have read the section above and be wondering: "OK, fine. But what happened later? Having got out of debt, did you start to slide back down the slippery slope into debt?"

So far so good, I'm glad to say. I'm still debt-free and solvent.

I'm now 71. I had never planned to retire, even before my financial crisis came along. I preferred the idea of reinvention. So

I have built up a portfolio career, which is a strategy I talk about in the book.

If you want to know what I'm up to these days, have a look at my blog at www.michaelmacmahon.com.

The National Picture

Before we go further, let's put things in context by looking briefly at the national picture.

Consumer debt has spiralled in recent years. When I was first writing this book, I decided to look at some comparisons. At that time, average UK household debt was £58,000 ($87,000) and total UK consumer debt was £1.46 trillion ($2.19 trillion).

That was slightly more than the UK's total income (GDP), which was then £1.396 trillion ($2.09 trillion), a figure I checked at the time with our Office of National Statistics (ONS).

A leading charity's website put it succinctly at the time: "Individuals owe more than what the whole country produces in a year."

The trend of increasing personal indebtedness, a by-product of our consumer culture, certainly contributed to the financial crisis. Yes, debt levels started to fall after the financial crisis but are rising again now. The country's GDP is on the rise again, so at the time of writing this edition it exceeds total personal indebtedness…but only slightly.

Most personal debt here is mortgage debt; and UK home ownership levels have traditionally been very high, though falling slightly since 2008. Is mortgage debt 'safe debt', as many people say? Yes, for as long as the housing market continued to rise; but at times of recession in the housing market, mortgages led borrowers into negative equity, where their property's value fell below the amount owing. Whenever these situations occur (and we can't be 100% sure they won't happen again), then mortgage debt does have to be factored into the equation.

Enough of the national background. What can you do about

your own debt situation? Hopefully the following pages will give you lots of ideas to use.

Note

References to legally binding arrangements apply primarily, but not exclusively, to the United Kingdom. As I've said many times elsewhere, the principles I outline for dealing with debt are universally applicable in my view; most of the content of this book is applicable wherever in the world you live.

Approximate US dollar equivalents (converted @ £1=$1.50) of any substantive monetary figures are given wherever appropriate.

And for 'pence in the pound', you can of course read 'cents in the dollar', 'cents in the euro', etc.

Causes of Debt

1

Perhaps you might think that this is not important. "I don't want to know why this happened: I just want to solve the problem." However, it's worthwhile to list some of the common causes of debt, if only so that you can see that debt is a widespread problem in our consumerist society. You don't need to be told that you are not the only person who has had this problem; but it might help to realise that you are a member of a very large club.

At the end of this section you'll find a few questions that could help trigger some thought processes for you.

We get into debt for a variety of reasons. The most common ones can be summarised as follows:

Major life events

- Getting married: the average wedding in the UK now costs over £20,000 ($30,000) and it is increasingly common for the couple themselves, rather than the bride's parents, to bear the cost. If this has to be borrowed, that's a sizeable debt with which to start married life.
- On the other side of the coin: divorce/relationship breakdown. Even if the split is amicable, with no financial disputes, the most obvious downside is that the people concerned previously needed only one home; now they need two.
- Job loss or business failure: again, two sides (employed or self-employed) of the same coin. Obviously the loss of one's primary or sole income is a major cause of debt

until rectified. What can make it worse is if suitable jobs/income cannot be found without moving, and if a property has to be sold the consequent delay adds to the income void.

- Ill-health, whether physical or mental in nature; also ill-health of partner, parent, child: private medical costs maybe; reduced/zero income maybe. In the worst cases, e.g. after a severe stroke, the partner might have to become a fulltime carer; therefore two incomes, not one, might disappear. Research shows that while one in eleven of the general population report debt problems, that rises to one in four of people with mental health problems and one in three of people with psychotic illnesses such as schizophrenia.

- Bereavement: especially significant if there are young children, thus limiting the earning potential of the surviving partner. Bereavement can be trebly debilitating from a financial viewpoint, with the possibility of reduced income, of increased costs, e.g. childcare or domestic help and, critically, an inability to deal with the situation because of grief.

Investments

- Property purchase: obviously the major purchase of most people's lives. In the UK, with the exception of occasional 'blips', this has usually been seen as a safe investment, until the global financial crisis of 2008 and consequent property downturn. The much-trumpeted recovery of the property market as this edition goes to print is focused mostly on the south-east; most of the rest of the country is still saying: "recovery? What recovery?" Even under normal market conditions, property purchase leads to liabilities, e.g. maintenance costs.

- Car purchase: to the extent that the car is needed for work, then this does indeed qualify as an investment.

- Educational costs of all kinds: including one's own

student loans; vocational training, etc. These all count as investments but can lead to significant debt.

Unbudgeted/Unexpected costs

- Mortgage repayment increases: the commonest cause here is an unexpected mortgage interest rate rise, which can lead to a debt buildup. Moreover many people, in order to get on to the property ladder, overstretch themselves while temporarily softening the pain by signing up to a discounted rate period. When that ends, with the inevitable 'tie-in' period that follows, debt can soon build up.
- Unexpected rent increases.
- Utility cost increases: the costs of energy and of water can fluctuate greatly. For those on fixed incomes, particularly, this can be a significant cause of debt.
- Local (especially indirect, not income-related) tax increases above the rate of inflation: the same applies as for utilities.
- Unexpected property maintenance costs; e.g. a property defect not covered by insurance. Which of us has the foresight or the spare cash to set up a contingency fund for maintenance? If you own an older property, this can be a significant issue; problems from roofs to drains and anything in between can lead to debt.

Discretionary spending (i.e. money you choose to spend)

- Holidays: good news while you're taking them but bad news when the credit card bill arrives, especially if boosted by fees for cash advances and currency transactions, mobile phone roaming charges, etc.
- Christmas: a time of 'comfort and joy'…but also of expensive peer pressure, if you have children. And increased food and drink spending for most of us.
- New clothes: retail therapy 'because I deserve it' seems extra-seductive when you are stressed by a debt problem.

- That beautiful car you've always fancied: so easy to convince yourself that it makes economic sense…and anyway you need a car to get to work. "The finance deal seemed good at the time." I've been there.
- Gambling: what starts as a small flutter can build up to a major debt problem.

Underpinning the above

As you'll see from the above list, which is by no means complete, there are many reasons why we might get into debt. At the end of the list, but very relevant because it's the major difference between economic facts now and in our parents' days, is 'because we can'. Ours is a 'spend now, pay later' culture. Moreover, in the nineties and the early years of the new millennium, credit was very easy to obtain. Under those conditions, the consequences of running unmanaged debt were less obvious, because there was always another attractive loan or credit card deal on offer. By the time you realised that you were in a hole, it was a deep one.

That's what happened to me when my business failed, as I outlined in 'My Story'. You might say that you haven't got a business. But you might have got into negative cash flow for the all-too-simple reason that you are spending more than your net income.

Negative cash flow is, of course, a fancy way of expressing what Mr Micawber was describing all those years ago.

In case you're not a fan of Dickens, Mr Micawber was a character from *David Copperfield*, who famously said, "Annual income twenty pounds, annual expenditure nineteen pounds nineteen shillings and sixpence, result happiness. Annual income twenty pounds, annual expenditure twenty pounds, ought and six, result misery."

Well, the story does not always end in misery, but it can.

By the way, "ought and six," means no shillings and six pence, in pre-decimal British currency; that's the equivalent of 2½ pence in today's currency. So the income/expenditure gap in Mr Micawber's homily was only 0.125%. One difference between

26

Dickens' day and ours is that people fall into debt with a gap between income and expenditure much more than 0.125%; but that gap would, in the recent days of easy credit, have been allowed to build up for several years before reality kicked in and produced, if not the debtors' court and the dreaded Marshalsea Prison of Dickens' days, then at least solicitors' letters. Some might contain threats of court action.

I hope this book will provide you with advice that will be of use to you and will get your thought processes going. It may then encourage you to think of other strategies that could work in your situation. Then you will have a 'virtuous circle' that can lift you out of the debt hole.

Self-diagnosis – a questionnaire

1   Do you know exactly how much you owe in total?
2   If you do, what is that total? How is it divided among your creditors?
3   If you don't know, when are you going to sit down with all those bank and credit card statements and work it out?
4   How does that total relate to your income? (i.e. how many weeks' or months' average take-home wage or salary?)
5   How does that total relate to your net assets (i.e. to the value of your home, if you own property, plus any other saleable assets, minus what you owe)?
6   Are you already receiving nasty letters from banks, credit card companies and other creditors? Or, if not, are you worried that they are just around the corner?
7   Do you know the interest rate(s) on your credit card(s)?
8   Are you making a regular payment of some sort against your credit card bill(s), even if it's not the amount they are asking for?
9   If not, could you do so?

Case studies

Peter Langley

Peter had a small business but longer hours were taking a toll on home life and his marriage began to fail. When he and his wife separated, he was struggling to support the business and also make maintenance payments and the cost of maintaining a second home. He soon found himself in debt. Meanwhile, Rose, who had always shared a car with Peter, now needed her own car for the school run and for work. Rose's major problem was housing; she had to take out a mortgage for the first time in her life in order to buy Peter out of his share in their home but she was overly optimistic about the financial position. In addition Peter's maintenance payments were variable because of the cash flow problems at his business; it's a well-known fact that problems in a relationship can lead to problems at work and vice-versa . Before long, one previously-solvent household had split into two debt-ridden households.

David Brown

David is an artist with a small and variable income and his wife Francesca was the family's main bread-winner. They were living a comfortable life in a village and sending their two children to private schools, until Francesca was afflicted by a chronic disease that prevented her working for several years. As they had a good credit history and lots of equity in their property, they had no difficulty in obtaining credit to maintain an unchanged lifestyle. Eventually, however, the long-standing nature of Francesca's illness and the credit crunch led to the bank pressurising the couple to clear their overdraft. They now had to accept that their previous lifestyle had become unsustainable. However, by this time the debts had built up to problem proportions and there was not enough income even to service the interest payments and certainly not enough to repay the capital.

Jane Greening

Jane has a debilitating condition that prevents her from working, so disability benefit is her only income. She had a friend who was a drug addict. One day she was too ill to go out and he said he'd go to the shops for her. Jane says: "I foolishly gave him my cash card and PIN number, because I trusted him. It was several days before I realised that he hadn't given the card back to me and by then he had withdrawn all the money from my account."

In addition the addict friend stole her cheque book and forged her signature on cheques, which then bounced. "It was an awful time; he'd betrayed me and spent all my money and left me to pick up the pieces. The companies involved – and the bank – said it was my fault and they were chasing me to pay for the goods that had been paid for with the bounced cheques."

Jane borrowed money from the bank to make up for the cash that had been stolen. However the interest on the loan was eating up all her benefits and she was unable to avoid going over her overdraft limit. Each letter from the bank, which informed her of what she already knew, was costing her £30 ($45).

"I found myself £3,000 ($4,500) in debt and I just didn't know what to do. My reaction was just to bury my head in the sand. I started to ignore the letters but, of course, all the time the debt keeps adding up. Eventually my landlord, who is, fortunately, a good friend, told me straight that I had to face up to the facts and do something about it."

Dan and Wendy Waring

Dan and Wendy had three young children; Dan was a skilled mechanic and Wendy was working night shifts as a nurse to boost their income and avoid childcare costs. Then Wendy, only 32, was struck down with an aggressive form of cancer and within a few months was dead.

Dan was in no psychological condition even to notice, let alone cope with, their rapidly deteriorating financial situation, devastated as he was by Wendy's illness and rapid decline. He was simply concentrating on trying to cope with his and the children's loss. The financial situation became worse when, in addition to the obvious loss of Wendy's income, Dan had to reduce his hours of work in order to do the school run, to be there for the children after school, etc, and he now had to pay for childcare for the youngest pre-school child. Dan also couldn't cope with shopping and housework on top of the school and nursery runs, so he had to employ domestic help. The combined effect of all these changes resulted in Dan's overdraft growing to massive proportions at a time of severely-reduced income. When the bank refused further credit, Dan turned to a local money-lender whose interest rates were astronomical. The result was a further deterioration in an already bad situation.

Nancy Sheppard

Nancy is a widow whose children had left home, so she was planning to move to a smaller property. In order to sell her house, she was forced to rectify a major defect with the drains. Nancy was on a small pension with no margin for eventualities but the repair bill was in the thousands, so she had to borrow the money. At the same time, the market had taken a downturn, so she had to accept a much lower price than expected for the house. This threw out Nancy's calculations for her purchase, to which she had committed before exchanging contracts on her sale; this left her with a debt that she could not repay out of income.

Nick Thompson

Nick, a single man, was given eight secured loans, and a mortgage, by the same bank. The total debt to the bank was £120,000 ($180,000) but his monthly salary is not enough to meet the repayments.

Nick also has a further £155,000 ($232,500) in unsecured lending, representing another 30 loans. It is thought that he will probably lose his home.

Fred Pollard

Fred had a monthly net income of £1,083 ($1,624), was given a loan on which repayments amount to £736 ($1,104), thus he had only £87 ($130) a week to live on. The local Citizens Advice Bureau (CAB) asked the lender if it had done checks – as required by the regulators – to ascertain that the loan was affordable. After a delay of four months, the bank responded by saying only that it had confirmed the income figure with Fred's employer.

Said the local Bureau manager: "The CAB will argue that debts should only be written off in cases such as the above, where loans had been made at the persistent suggestion of bank staff to people who clearly could not afford them, were confused and should never have been offered them."

Ben Fielding

Ben has bipolar disorder. His bank increased credit limits on a regular basis, although they had been asked by Ben and his wife to reduce them. By the time the credit crunch forced everyone to face facts the debts had built up to £75,000 ($112,500). It is noted that the incidence of debt problems is much higher in people with mental illness than in the population at large.

Janice Summerfield

Janice has schizophrenia; she lives solely on benefits and is too ill to work. Despite this, she had been given credit of £14,000 ($21,000); moreover her credit limits had been raised on a regular basis without notice. Another all-too-common example of mental illness leading to increased financial problems.

"Possessions are generally diminished by possession." – Nietzsche

Finally...

We get into debt for all sorts of reasons. For example:

Major Life Events

- Getting married.
- Divorce/relationship breakup.
- Job loss or business failure.
- Ill-health, physical or mental.
- Bereavement.

Investments

- Property purchase.
- Car purchase. (Where necessary for work or family commitments.)
- Educational costs.

Unexpected Costs

- Mortgage repayment increases.
- Rent increases.
- Utility cost increases.
- Local tax increases.
- Property maintenance costs.

Discretionary Spending

- Holidays.
- Christmas.
- Entertainment.
- Gambling.
- Clothes; other goods you want but don't need.
- That wonderful sports car you've always fancied.

And underneath it all…easy credit when it's available, as it was pre-2008 and doubtless will be again; and peer pressure, which will always be with us.

"The idea that money doesn't buy happiness is a lie put about by the rich, to stop the poor from killing them." – Michael Caine

Mind Over Matter 2

How to reduce the stress caused by debt

Before we get on to the practical issues surrounding dealing with debt, there is a vitally important aspect of indebtedness: the importance of mindset, or mental attitude.

Being in debt increases stress: that's obvious to everyone who has been in that situation. How we react to that stress greatly influences our success or otherwise in getting out of debt. Sometimes we seek external aids; we might drink more than we usually do, as I did. If we are smokers then we might smoke more, or if we are ex-smokers we might start again, as I did. Increased drug use of all kinds can be related to debt. However, the stress relief we might get from these is only temporary, and costs money, which is not what we want. There is a better and more long-lasting way to manage stress, which is to use our knowledge of how our minds and brains work.

Napoleon Hill, an early writer on the habits and characteristics of successful people, wrote, "In my youth, when I worked as a bank clerk, (this was back in the early 20th century, when credit was hard to come by) I could tell, before a man was 10 feet inside the bank door, whether he expected to get his cheque cashed."

What he didn't say was that less-confident customers probably had their accounts scrutinised more closely before being given any cash. Thus being confident, or at least appearing to be confident, might have helped some of his customers to get cash or, in effect, to get credit despite their accounts not being 'in the black'.

"That's all very well," I hear you say; "getting credit has not been my problem. That's been easy; now I need to get out of the hole that easy credit got me into." My contention, however, is that exactly the same principle applies here. On my wall is a slogan: "Act as if…" and it has served me well over the years whenever I was in a difficult situation. It's a very adaptable, multipurpose slogan, meaning that if you act as if things are going well, or are about to go well, then you increase the chances that they will. Let's call it the power of positive expectations.

You might well say that confidence, or maybe over-confidence, or excessively positive expectations, led you to the debt problem you have now. That may or may not be true but your prospects of getting out of this situation are greatly increased if you can manage to remain positive.

My daughters used to laugh about the fact that I always seemed to find a parking space, because I always believed I would (nowadays I don't run a car, so I don't need a parking space). My explanation was that because I believed I'd find one, I was relaxed about it, thus when a space became free I'd see it quickly. It's said that if you are stressed (even about something relatively trivial, such as a parking space) part of your brain shuts down; it's part of the so-called 'fight or flight' reflex.

There is a more scientific demonstration of the power of positive expectations, which is sometimes called 'The Harvard Experiment' because, although it was carried out in California, it was devised by a Harvard academic, Robert Rosenthal.

The power of positive expectations

The Harvard Experiment demonstrates the value of positive expectations; of ourselves and of others.

This is because our interactions with others reflect our beliefs about ourselves; other people, if they are perceptive, pick up quickly what we think of ourselves and what we expect to happen. Surprising as it seemed when I first heard this theory, they will often try to behave consistently with what they perceive our expectations of them to be.

There is other evidence of this so-called 'expectations theory' in the psychology literature: the serious as well as the more popular versions. In case that kind of stuff is not your favourite bedtime reading, this summary of the Harvard Experiment is practical proof: something which sets an example that should be (but is not) followed in every school in the world.

Dr Rosenthal conducted the experiment in 1968, in a school in the San Francisco Bay area. His theory was that children could become brighter when expected to by their teachers and he conducted a study to test the theory. All of the children in the study were administered a nonverbal test of intelligence, disguised as a test that would predict intellectual 'blooming'.

There were 18 classrooms in the school, three at each of the six grade levels. Within each grade level, the three classrooms were composed of children with above-average ability, average ability, and below-average ability, respectively.

Within each of the 18 classrooms, approximately 20% of the children were chosen at random to form the experimental group. The teachers of these children were told that their pupils' scores on the 'Test of Inflected Acquisition' indicated they would show surprising gains in intellectual competence during the next eight months of school. The only difference between the experimental groups and the remainder was in the minds of the teachers. At the end of the school year all the children were retested with the same test of intelligence. Overall, the children from whom the teachers had been led to expect greater intellectual gain showed a significantly greater gain than did the children in the control group. (If you want more info, you can do a search under Rosenthal & Jacobson, 1968).

Rosenthal's work showed that having high expectations of others can influence their performance in a positive way and to a significant degree.

However, there is one further point worthy of repetition. The only difference between the experimental group and the remainder was in the minds of the teachers. That "experimental group" of students, as Rosenthal calls them, was chosen at random. When this fact was revealed to the teachers at the end of the experiment, they were amazed because not only were the measurable results better, but they also reported other benefits, e.g. "behaviour was better; no disciplinary problems; it was a pleasure to teach!" The teachers then assumed that the remarkable results were because of their previously-known teaching performance. "No doubt," said the principal, "but you were chosen at random too."

Have the important role models in your life had high expectations of you? I hope they have. I was lucky to have three very positive role models in my younger life; my father Patrick MacMahon, my headmaster Fr Peter Murtough and one of my first bosses, Peter Mossop. All three had high implicit and explicit expectations of me, so I am sure that my behaviour reflected that (well, sometimes, anyway). All are now, sadly, dead. But whenever I am faced with a tricky situation I can ask myself: "what would PM have advised?"

The corollary of this is that I believe that the things that happen in my life are very much influenced by what I expect to happen. Muhammad Ali was famous for saying, "I am the greatest", but he used to say it even before he was the Olympic champion, before he turned professional and became world champion. We in the UK are more reticent about proclaiming our talents, our strengths, our virtues, but there is a lesson to be learned from Ali.

The moral is this: I believe that if you expect something good to happen, it is more likely to happen, if that outcome depends to any significant extent on your interaction with others…as many outcomes do.

A traveller arrived at the gates of a city in the 14th century.

Before entering, he asked the gatekeeper: "What are the people like here?"

The gatekeeper replied: "What were they like where you came from?"

"They were wonderful people: they were friendly and generous and would share their last crust of bread with you", said the traveller.

"You will find them the same here."

A second traveller arrived and asked the gatekeeper the same question.

"What were they like where you came from?" said the gatekeeper.

"They were terrible people: they would steal from you at the slightest chance."

"I am afraid you will find them the same here," replied the wise gatekeeper.

An extension of this story is that while you are negotiating with your creditors, if you show that you expect to be debt-free in a given time, and that you'll do whatever it takes to get there, and if you are persistent in acting that way, eventually you'll find people who will help you. They may be employees or managers in the very companies to whom you owe money; they are just people doing a job, after all.

Why not decide what you want and act as if it were already a reality? Then three things could happen. One, you attract people who can help, as said above. Two, you get where you want, faster. Three, and most importantly, you preserve your health and sanity.

As I said above, positive expectations seem to me the best strategy when the outcome depends partly or wholly on you. If you have no influence on the outcome (tomorrow's weather; that movie you're going to see; a meal in that new restaurant?) then positive expectations could lead to disappointment. You will probably hope for the best; but being detached from the outcome is probably better. I'll never forget a rotten evening I had at the theatre once, simply because my expectations were sky-high.

A wise woman who used to be President of the nationwide organisation of Women's Institutes in the UK had on her wall the following motto: "Hope for the best. Prepare for the worst. Take what comes."

But – and it's a big but, so it's worth repetition – if the

outcome depends partly or wholly on your input and your interaction with others, then positive expectations seem to me the way to go. As Winston Churchill said (at a time when most things in this country and maybe even in the world were directly or indirectly influenced by him): "I am an optimist. It does not seem too much use being anything else."

Stress

Back to the beginning: how can we use our knowledge of how the mind works in order to help us in those first difficult days, when we have started to realise the situation in its entirety: when we have moved on from being in denial about our debt problem but we don't yet have a plan?

Or, to misquote Kipling: "If you can keep your head when all around you are losing theirs...you don't understand the situation." Seriously though, this is a time when a little knowledge of your own thought processes can alleviate the worst effects of stress... and stress is a natural consequence of being seriously in debt.

We all experience stress at various times and a certain amount of it is positive; without it we wouldn't get out of bed most days. What I'm talking about here is called in the jargon 'distress' and it's the right word.

It is sometimes said that the conscious mind can only hold one thought at a time. Buried in our *sub*conscious mind, however, are millions of pieces of data. Some people liken the subconscious mind to the processor of a PC, and the conscious mind to the monitor or screen. Others prefer the analogy of an iceberg: what percentage is below the surface? Some of that data will be facts, some of it impressions or feelings, such as how you felt when you saw that final demand notice on your doormat. Sadly, it is hard or impossible to control the way thoughts pop up from the subconscious mind on to the monitor of your conscious mind. If those thoughts are predominantly negative, then you will be stressed all the time. But, remember, the conscious mind can only hold one thought at a time. That thought might switch frequently if you have a butterfly mind, but you can help it along. How? By choosing to populate your conscious mind with a clear mental picture of what you want to happen, not what you fear.

On the other hand, you may have heard it said that 'managing expectations' means creating low expectations in others, which can easily be exceeded. For example, many theme parks have signs telling you how long you'll have to wait in line from a specific point. It's well known that Disney states these times in a pessimistic way, so that the visitors will feel pleased that they got to the front of the line faster than they had expected. The same is true in managing expectations in one's boss. I had an American colleague who, every year, had major fights with his boss to negotiate more realistic (i.e. lower) sales targets. "I decided," said Carl, "that I'd rather have a fight once a year at target-setting time, than have a fight every month-end." In other words he managed his boss's expectations downwards. That is fine for creating and managing the expectations of your boss or, dare I say it, your clients. But in managing your own expectations – and those of others with whom you interact while you are dealing with your debts – I hope you'll agree with me that positive expectations are the way to go.

Creating your own space

The life of the late Seve Ballesteros has recently (2014) been celebrated in a movie biopic. The inspirational Spanish golfer used to tell a story about how he developed a technique to protect himself from the negative thoughts of others, a technique that you might find useful in this as in other challenges in your life. "I realised that when I played an important match all the other golfers, all their back-up teams and families all wanted me to play badly. I became so aware of these negative thoughts that it began to affect my game."

What did Seve do? Simple; he decided to carry a bubble around with him. "Every time I stepped up to hit a shot, I imagined that I was stepping into a large bubble. Once inside, I was protected against the negative wishes of others".

Could you borrow something from Seve's idea? At certain points in your debt-management process, you will almost certainly be bombarded with payment reminders, final demands and the full panoply of the financial services industry's 'collection services'. You may even receive these communications as frequently as the offers of new credit cards and increased credit limits that you used to receive in the past – until the credit crunch and until the lenders realised that you had finally made the decision 'enough is enough' and had decided to reduce your debts rather than routinely 'revolving' them. By the way, did you know that the card company might have actually called you just that? Someone who only pays the minimum amount each month is called a 'revolver'. If that's what you did, you were exactly the client group they targeted. But that was then. You know better now.

Maybe Seve's bubble idea doesn't work for you, so here's a modification. Jack Black, the wise and witty Scottish author and trainer, has upgraded Seve's bubble and he carries around an imaginary bell-jar. Any potentially stressful situation and he says to himself, "Bell-jar…ON!!" and then the 'slings and arrows of outrageous fortune' cannot harm him.

If, on the other hand, you are the kind of logical, 'left-brain' kind of person who would find the idea of personal bubbles or bell-jars – virtual or not – too off-the wall, here's a practical strategy that can achieve the same results.

In order to create space between you and your creditors, I recommend that you conduct your negotiations in writing only. There are all kinds of benefits here:

- You have time to think before responding.
- It will look professional; if you are not good at composing letters, there are some examples in the 'resources' section, which you can adapt to fit your situation; or you can get an adviser to help.
- You have a record of everything that has been said by both parties.
- …and most importantly, it is less stressful.

'Let the answering machine take the strain'

Follow this strategy, summon up your reserves of patience and persistence, and the huge benefit is that you avoid verbal discussions. They are just too stressful right now and, thanks to that wonderful invention the telephone answering machine, you need never speak to a creditor in person.

When I say this, I am not advocating that you ignore telephone calls. No, I feel you should respond if a creditor leaves a message but you do it in writing, referring to any previous correspondence and repeating your previous offer, if you have made one, or perhaps making an offer, if you have not done so. Alternatively you could simply state your position and ask for their understanding and for more time.

One slight disadvantage of the telephone 'bubble' concept (Seve Ballesteros again) could be that your friends might notice that you are never in, even when they expected you to be so. Is that a major problem? Probably not. If you have an actual answering machine, rather than the service from your telephone provider, then you can use it to filter your calls, by listening to the machine before deciding whether to pick up. If you have 'caller display' on your home phone, or you are being called on a mobile, problem solved: you can be 100% selective about which calls you accept and which you allow to go through to voicemail.

Now I do recognise that there are some people who simply cannot resist answering a ringing phone. If you are one of those people and you can't break the habit, then all I can say is that I hope you are someone who is not stressed out by this kind of situation, in which case you are in the lucky minority. In such a case, carry on following your instincts and answer the phone, but I would still urge you not to conduct a negotiation on the phone. Simply take in what is said and offer to think it over and reply – but in writing.

Always respond both to written correspondence and to phone messages and do so Promptly, Politely, Professionally and Persistently (i.e. sticking to your guns). Forgive my alliteration: I'm pretty sure it'll help you to remember the strategy.

In the Resources section at the end of the book there are some examples of letter formats you could customise to your situation.

Harassment

In the UK, it is illegal for creditors to harass debtors. The Government's Office of Fair Trading developed the following definitions of harassment, which are now enforced by the FCA.

Physical/psychological harassment: putting pressure on debtors or third parties is considered to be oppressive. Examples of unfair practices are as follows:

- Contacting debtors at unreasonable times and at unreasonable intervals.
- Pressurising debtors to sell property, to raise funds by further borrowing or to extend their borrowing.
- Using more than one debt collection business at the same time resulting in repetitive and/or frequent contact by different parties.
- Not ensuring that an adequate history of the debt is passed on as appropriate resulting in repetitive and/or frequent contact by different parties.
- Not informing the debtor when their case has been passed on to a different debt collector.
- Pressurising debtors to pay in full, in unreasonably large instalments, or to increase payments when they are unable to do so.
- Making threatening statements or gestures or taking actions which suggest harm to debtors.
- Ignoring and/or disregarding claims that debts have been settled or are disputed and continuing to make unjustified demands for payment.
- Disclosing or threatening to disclose debt details to third parties unless legally entitled to do so.
- Acting in a way likely to be publicly embarrassing

to the debtor either deliberately or through lack of care, for example, by not putting correspondence in a sealed envelope and putting it through a letterbox, thereby running the risk that it could be read by third parties.

Note

The OFT closed down on 1 April 2014 and its responsibilities for consumer protection in the UK, including enforcement of the above guidelines, passed to the Financial Conduct Authority (FCA) with effect from that date. For the up-to-date position, consult Citizens Advice.

"There are many things in life that are more important than money. And they all cost money." – Fred Allen

Finally...

- Our thoughts influence our behaviour, which influences our results.
- It's vitally important to stay positive when facing a debt crisis.
- 'Act as if' you'll be able to work your way out of this situation – and act that way consistently and persistently – and your behaviour will influence your creditors.
- Henry Ford: "If you think you can, or you think you can't, you're probably right."
- 'The Harvard Experiment': the students were chosen at random, so were the teachers. The improved results were achieved because the teachers *believed* the children were more gifted than average.
- The traveller at the gate: "I think you'll find they are the same here."
- To minimise stress: create a clear positive picture of the result you want. Then keep it in the forefront of your mind.

- Create your own space: Seve Ballesteros and the bubble. Eliminate the negative influences of other people's thoughts.
- Conduct all negotiations in writing. Avoid discussing on the phone: if you must answer it, simply note what is said, refer to previous correspondence, if any, and then respond…but in writing, not on the phone.
- Beware: letters apparently from 'solicitors' and 'debt collection companies' are sometimes really from the creditor. A neat tactic to put extra pressure on you without them having to go to the trouble and cost of involving third parties.
- Harassing debtors is illegal. If it happens to you, get help immediately. You can make a complaint to Trading Standards (via Consumer Direct, 08454 04 05 06), to the police if the harassment is severe or, if it is your landlord demanding money, your local council.
- Rules for correspondence: Prompt (replying). Polite, Professional & Persistent. ("If at first you don't succeed, try, try and try again.")
- …and finally finally…don't keep it to yourself. Many people in debt crisis (men particularly) avoid sharing the problem. I was one of them. It's understandable; but unwise.

"If I can't take it with me, I refuse to go." – Jack Benny

A Coach's Approach to Dealing with Debt

3

Coaches and debt counsellors know that questions have power, so their 'mental toolkits' are full of questions. The idea is that if the right questions are asked, then the client (that's you) has, or will find, the knowledge and resources to deal with the situation. As I myself am a coach, I believe this approach is more effective than the client being told what to do.

However, coaches also know that in difficult situations their clients sometimes do need to be advised what to do next; stress makes decision-making hard, if not impossible, and a debt crisis can be a massive cause of stress. Thus the experienced coach or debt counsellor *can* give advice, or at least suggest some options. But in the long term he or she will prefer that you make the decisions and find the solutions yourself, with prompting by the right questions.

The classic coaching process is described by the acronym GROW. It can be summarised as follows:

- **G**oal: exactly what do you want to achieve?
- **R**eality: exactly what is your current situation?
- **O**ptions: how could you get to where you want to be? (There may be several different options.)
- **W**ay forward: what will you do? When? What's the next step? This forms your plan of action.

Goal

The first step is to define *exactly* what you want to achieve.

Reality

After defining your goal(s), next comes current reality: a detailed analysis of your financial situation at this moment, listing all your liabilities, i.e. debts; your bank balance; also your current income and expenditure; and finally your assets.

Two things to say about doing the reality check at this point. Firstly, some people have said to me, "shouldn't I do the reality check first?" The answer is no; it is usually better to set a goal first, then look at where you are now, then decide how to bridge the gap. If you look at reality first, you might be so depressed that you never set a goal.

Secondly, you may be pleasantly surprised, not by the figures themselves, but because writing down the 'reality' figures in detail – and all the work of going through bank and credit card statements that you'll need to do first – reduces the stress of the situation, compared with that vague 'sword of Damocles' feeling of threat that has maybe existed for months, during which time you knew you were in a tight spot but didn't know exactly how tight. You've probably heard of Taoist philosopher Lao-Tzu's famous saying, "A journey of a thousand miles begins with a single step"; it is also sometimes said that the greatest stress in life is caused by inaction owing to unmade decisions. When you have decided your goal(s) and analysed your reality, you have made the first decision and have started on the path to action.

Options

Defining your goals and reality will show you the size of the gap to be bridged. This is the time to brainstorm (alone or with a friend or adviser) to find the options for bridging the gap. Chapter 6 suggests a way of conducting this exercise. The purpose of brainstorming is to develop the maximum number of ideas on the chosen topic, with a totally open mind, i.e. a stream of consciousness before your inner critic kicks in and starts saying "that won't work." Then, and only then, do you begin to evaluate the various options and start to formulate your plan.

Way forward (what, when, etc.)

"The best-laid schemes o' mice an' men gang aft agley," as the Scottish poet Burns tells us. "Gang aft agley", of course, means they often go wrong. Setting a goal, analysing current reality and then developing some options to bridge the gap are necessary but not sufficient. Obviously, without action those goals will remain just pipe-dreams. So the next step is to make a practical plan, which is no more nor less than a list of actions, prioritised and with deadlines.

Questions are powerful; and perhaps the most powerful of all are the 'W-questions'. What will you do? When? Who can help you? Etc, etc.

But for the time being, forget the 'why' question; that's more to do with the reasons you got into debt. That's the past; you are dealing with the present and the future.

So you need to ask yourself all those questions and then act on the answers.

The influence of belief is important here too. What do you think is the likelihood that you will complete each of the steps in your plan? If you are not sure that you *will* complete all the steps, then think again. It may be better to re-cast your plan: modify the goal perhaps, or, more likely, give yourself more time. When goals are not attained it is often the case that the goal was the right one but the timeframe was unrealistic.

Finally...

It helps to achieve a satisfactory outcome – AND reduce stress whilst doing it – if you inject some structure, i.e. have a plan. The structure used by many coaches is described as follows:

- **G**oal: exactly what do you want to achieve?
- **R**eality: evaluate and describe (in writing, in detail) your current situation.
- **O**ptions: make a list of all the possible ways you could get where you want to be.

- **W**ay forward: this is decision time. Which option(s) will you choose? What will you do? When? Who can help you? This is the basis of your plan of action.

"Imagination is more important than knowledge." – Einstein

Goals

4

What do you want to achieve? By when?

So, as your imaginary coach will say, the very first thing to do is to decide what your goal is. In other words: when you have dealt with your debt situation to your own satisfaction, what do you want to have achieved?

You might well simply say: "to have solved my debt problem," but is this specific enough? For example, if you state the goal in that way, how will you know when you have got there? The goal-setting experts (and there are many of them) all agree that you need to be more precise. For example: by how much do you want to reduce your debt? To zero? By 50%? By what date? The New Year? Your next birthday?

If you are new to this goal-setting thinking and are interested enough to learn more, there are plenty of books on the subject. And at the end of this chapter you'll find a checklist to help set a goal on this or any other topic.

Goals, according to many of those same goal-setting experts, need to be:

- **S**pecific: Goals that are vaguely stated are usually not achieved.
- **M**easurable: There is a saying in business, "what cannot be measured cannot be managed" and that's to a large extent true for personal goals too.
- **A**chievable: The experts say that a goal should be challenging but should also be achievable; that's a difficult balance, of course. Setting goals that seem to

be unachievable is very demotivating. Well, it is for most of us, though it's what turns super-achievers on.

- **R**elevant: Is the goal consistent with your values? To give an extreme example, if you can only achieve a certain financial goal by being economical with the truth, and if that behaviour is not your style, then you probably won't work effectively towards that goal.

To give a less extreme example, if your favoured recovery plan would involve big reductions in spending on Christmas presents/meals out etc, which you think will make your partner or children unhappy, and if your so-called 'hierarchy of values' puts their material happiness above all else, then you have an obvious conflict between this goal and your values, which needs addressing.

- **T**ime-Bounded: By what date do you want to achieve the goal?

It's often said that people who are goal-oriented tend to achieve more than most people because it's better to focus on where you want to get to, rather than focussing on your problems.

Examples

A debt-related goal might simply be an amount of money and a date, for example:

- "To have reduced my total debts to £xxxx (or $xxxx or €xxxx) by the New Year."

…or it could be relative to some other measure of your financial reality. Here are two examples:

- "To have reduced my credit-card debt to three months' net income, within six months."

- "To have reduced my total debt (i.e. including mortgage) to 25% of my net worth, by the New Year." Net worth is a snapshot of your economic position, expressed as the value of all your assets – i.e. everything you own – minus the value of all your liabilities – i.e. everything you owe.

Therefore your goal might be a certain amount of money but it might alternatively be a percentage, or a multiple, of one of your other financial realities.

I mentioned the received wisdom that goals must be specific, measurable, achievable, relevant and finally time-bounded, in other words: "by what date will you achieve it?" When a goal is not achieved, it is often because insufficient time was allowed, not because the goal was wrong.

Writing it down

Already you will see that this process requires a lot of thought and it requires a notepad and a pen, even before you have started sorting through those bank statements and credit card bills that you have been ignoring for months. Starting to work on paper has, for many people including myself, a calming influence in itself. Writing down your situation in detail takes away some of those vague feelings of threat, no matter how bad the facts are.

I have suggested previously that for this goal-setting step you try to work out what you want your goal to be, before, not after, you have analysed your current reality. That might seem counterintuitive but it's why I have put the chapters in this order. The very act of setting a goal should inspire you to action; you'll be in a better frame of mind if you do so before you sit down with all your financial records to analyse your current reality.

When you have decided your goal, writing it down is helpful; some say it's essential. We are, of course, all different in the way we approach situations. You might decide your goal, write it in simple and straightforward language on a piece of paper (maybe the proverbial 'back of an envelope'), and stick it on the fridge door where you can see it every day. If you are of a more analytical persuasion you might like the following method.

Goal-setting steps: the long version

1   Before you start: do you really want to change this aspect of your life? Is the achievement of this goal really important to you? (Be personal and selfish for this purpose.) I take it that if you're reading this book the answer to this question will be yes.

2   Decide what the goal is. Write it down in detail, in the present tense, including a measure of how you'll know the goal has been achieved.

3   Belief – do you believe that you have the ability to achieve the goal? The goal must be challenging and stretching and must cause you to move out of your comfort zone; but you must also believe that you can achieve it. Can you create a mental picture of it already achieved?

4   Values check: does the achievement of this goal fit your value system? This is an important question for goal-setting in general.

5   Benefits: make a list of ways in which *you personally* will benefit from the goal's attainment. The more reasons, the more easily will you find energy and motivation.

6   Analyse your present position. See chapter 5 of this book.

7   Set a deadline for the attainment of the goal. If, as is generally the case, achieving the goal will take some time, break it down into steps and specify the intermediate deadlines too.

8   Develop a list of strategic options (not actions), i.e. what possible routes could you take to get to your goal from where you are now?

9   Identify any obstacles which might have to be overcome. Sometimes just making the list will lessen your perception of the threats.

10 Identify what extra information, if any, you will need in

order to attain the goal. Decide how and when you will get hold of this information.

11 Identify any people or groups whose co-operation and support you might need. Is there anything you can do for them in return for their support?

12 Make a plan. List all the activities and prioritise them. Which is most important, which is most urgent, which will you do first? Continually go back and review the plan.

13 Get a clear mental image (a visualisation) that represents the goal as if it were already attained. Every time you have a spare moment, play that picture on the screen of your mind.

14 Develop an affirmation, i.e. a description of your future reality, which you can say to yourself from time to time. Follow the example of Mohammed Ali. His most famous affirmation was: "I'm the greatest!" Yours, for example, might be: "my finances are in good shape again," or: "I'm back to the black!"

15 Manage your time effectively on a day-to-day basis; prioritise actions. Get in the habit of doing something towards the goal every day.

Maybe steps 13 and 14 (visualisation and affirmations) are a little too far-out for you. They used to be too far-out for me, as I was a logical 'left-brain type'. I now realise that things like this can work.

"Those are my principles. If you don't like them, I have others."
– Groucho Marx

Finally

- Set your goals: to clear your debts to zero? Or to get them down to a certain figure? or to a certain number of months' income? Or to a certain percentage of your net worth, if you have calculated that? And by what date do you want to do it?

- Write the goal down.
- Values check: your goal(s) must be consistent with your values.
- When you set your goals, remember the salami principle. Salami in thin slices is more appetising than the entire sausage. Slice the goal into several smaller and less daunting steps, put a date on each, and hey presto, you have a plan. (There is a less appealing version of this principle: "anyone can eat an elephant: one bite at a time".)

"You don't understand. It's not the principle. It's the money."
– Tommy Cooper, arguing with a barman over his change.

Reality

5

Facing facts, analysing your financial situation

You have started out in a positive way by defining your debt-related goal. Now it's time for the reality check, where your virtual coach will ask you to be tough with yourself.

This second stage of your personal debt recovery process will produce an accurate picture of your current reality in financial terms. Maybe you have been sweeping 'those letters' under the mat or throwing them away; now you need to start opening them. First you must set aside a good chunk of time to accumulate and sort out bank statements, credit card bills, etc.

This job can be done in your home office, or at your kitchen table: anywhere you have space to spread out all the papers you need. Much as I love working in cafes, this isn't one of those projects that lends itself to that kind of venue; anyway, drinking coffee at home costs much less. It'd be a good idea to get a lever-arch file for all related correspondence while you're dealing with your debts. Because, whatever you decide to do, you'll need time. Negotiating for that extra time will need correspondence.

Getting help

You don't need to go through this process alone. In this book I refer frequently to an imaginary coach or debt counsellor and the questions such a person might ask you. There are lots of real professionals out there, many of whom will help you for free. See the Resources section if you don't know where to find an adviser.

Can a piece of paper kill you?

Jack Black asks a (rhetorical?) question in one of his seminars: "can a piece of paper kill you?" He goes on to describe the following scenario: a brown envelope arrives on your doormat. You sweep it under the carpet, metaphorically speaking. But you can't really ignore it: the fact of its arrival, your guess at the contents, plus the fact you haven't opened it and thus don't know the contents for sure, but you assume the worst, has now embedded itself in your subconscious. As Black says, the conscious mind can only hold one thought at a time but thoughts pop up from our subconscious in a way that is hard to control. (Not impossible to control, but hard.)

In this scenario, the random thoughts are probably stress-inducing.

As more of these envelopes arrive and are ignored, the stress builds up in the pressure-cooker of your subconscious mind. The memory of all those envelopes will pop up when you are least expecting it; you might be at home or you might be overtaking a truck at 80 mph on the motorway. The result could be a crash, a heart attack, a stroke, or a combination of those.

Those brown envelopes that could kill you are repayment demands from creditors – although many of them use better-quality white envelopes these days to get your attention.

Opening a letter won't kill you

It might have been Goethe (did he have debt problems? I must check) who said that one of the greatest causes of stress is the postponement of a decision that you know you must make. I agree, provided that you have the information that you need to make the decision, and that's what we are doing here.

The moral of the Goethe quote, and of Jack Black's story, is this: OPEN those envelopes, read and note the contents, then decide what you are going to do about each one. This is particularly so for the taxman, because those guys never go away. You may have heard the old joke, "What's the difference between a Jewish mother and a Rottweiler? The Rottweiler eventually lets go". Well, the taxman is in the Jewish mother category. I found that all my other creditors were prepared to negotiate a partial payment, except the Revenue: all the taxman would agree to was extra time to pay, plus freezing surcharges and interest for late payment. At the time I was technically self-employed, even though my income was very small, so the Revenue's view was that I could pay my income tax arrears in full from future earnings, even if it might take years. They also allowed me to pay back my VAT arrears in full over about 10 years. If you are unemployed, however, they might take a different view and 'forgive' some of the debt.

Sorting that paperwork

The kinds of documents you need first will be those that allow you to add up your total debts/liabilities:

1   Bank statements: do you have an overdraft? How much?
2   Credit card and store card statements.
3   Invoices, bills, etc from other creditors.
4   Tax correspondence, especially if you are self-employed.
5   Estimates of 'informal' liabilities, e.g. any unpaid loans from friends or family.

When you have totalled all the debts in categories 1-5 and are sure that you have gone as far as you can go in recording your current liabilities, i.e. your total debts, now put the situation in perspective by listing the positive side of your 'personal balance sheet', i.e.

6   Up-to-date estimates of the value of your assets, e.g. property; car; cash at bank (if your account is in the black); shares; insurance policies; money owed to you, including refunds; occupational pension funds [if you are old enough to be able to cash them in]; valuables, e.g. jewellery, antiques etc; and anything that could be turned into cash 'if push came to shove'.

Now sort out and prioritise your debts, as follows:

- **Priority:** roof-over-your-head and essential utilities, for example:

    - Mortgage or rent arrears (you could lose your home).
    - Any other debts secured on your home (same result).
    - Council Tax (they can send in the bailiffs).
    - Gas & electricity (they can cut you off).
    - Water (though you cannot be cut off by the law in the UK).

- **Non-priority**: other services you need, e.g. car loan; home or mobile phone; credit cards; all other creditors.

Regarding unsecured debts, credit cards, etc, what is the lender's recourse? Stop giving you more credit, (maybe a good idea) or take you to court? How likely they are to take you to court depends on the amount you owe, as there are costs for the lender.

Update your list regularly. Any reduction in the total you owe, even small, is good for your peace of mind.

Non-financial assets

The accountants amongst us would say that 'assets' means only your financial assets. That's fine, but I would go further: list also any other assets which could be of use, for example skills and talents which you are not using but which might help you to generate cash. What about people you know who might have expertise, experience or contacts that might help you solve your debt challenge?

Spending a little time to assess your 'non-financial assets' is valuable, not only because it will give you more in the 'options' column but because it will make you feel better than you would feel if you simply focussed on the problem.

Income and expenditure

Now that you have assessed not only your liabilities/debts but also your assets, you need to evaluate the current situation as regards income and expenditure. It's a 'profit and loss statement' for your life, based on your current spending pattern. That might be something you are fully aware of; you might be someone who can write down the key numbers from memory (one of the most successful businessmen I've ever met told me that he didn't believe in any business plan that couldn't be written on the back of an envelope).

However, many of us (myself included) do not have instant recall of these important figures; that could be one of the reasons we ended up with a debt problem. Therefore some kind of aide-memoire is necessary: a table into which you insert the key figures. If you have sought support from a money adviser of some kind, then it's likely that you were immediately given an income and expenditure sheet to complete. Any debt adviser, independent or not, will be happy to give you a suitable form; they are sometimes called 'Statements of Affairs'.

Key ratios

Finally you need to get the picture in perspective: analyse your total debt relative to your income and your assets. For example, what multiple of your net monthly income does your total debt represent? Or what percentage of your net worth? These are what I call your personal 'key ratios' and your goals might well relate to a key ratio rather than a monetary figure.

When you have assembled, on paper or on your computer, this comprehensive summary of your key financial data, you will be in a better position to start developing your options, i.e. the possible solutions. Then, and only then, will you be in a good position to choose the solution that will work for you.

Disposable and discretionary income

A key question in dealing with debt is this: what is your disposable or discretionary income? What is left after tax and essential expenditure? Note I said after essential expenditure, not what's left after your customary expenditure, because the answer to the latter question is probably zero or a negative figure, which is why you have a debt problem.

You'll find more on discretionary income in Chapters 7 and 8, because if you believe you can pay every debt in full, within a timeframe that's acceptable to your creditors, then you will have to find a way to maximise your discretionary income. That will probably involve making more ruthless distinctions between what's essential and what's been customary up to now. Or, to put it another way, between what is essential to *life* and what you have previously seen as essential to your *lifestyle*.

Words from the wise

In his classic book, *How to Stop Worrying and Start Living*, Dale Carnegie proposed that we apply the following sequence when making decisions:

> First – Get all the facts. To quote Dean Hawkes of Columbia University, "half the worry in the world is caused by people trying to make decisions before they have sufficient knowledge on which to base a decision." You need to define the problem, determine the cause of the problem, and come up with a list of all the possible solutions you can think of.

> Second – Carefully weigh all of the facts and then come to a decision. Ask yourself: "What is the best solution?"

> Third – Once a decision is carefully reached, act! Get busy carrying out your decision–and dismiss all anxiety about the outcome.

Carnegie was the author of one of the best-selling books of all time (*How to Win Friends and Influence People*), so who am I to disagree?

"Who steals my purse steals trash; 'tis something, nothing;
'Twas mine, 'tis his, and has been slave to thousands;
But he that filches from me my good name
Robs me of that which not enriches him,
And makes me poor indeed." – Shakespeare

Finally...

- Don't sweep the letters under the mat.
- Set aside time to accumulate bank statements, credit card bills, etc.
- Making a detailed list of all debts lessens the stress.
    - List your debts and prioritise them as follows: priority: roof-over-your-head and essential utilities, e.g. mortgage or rent arrears (you could lose your home); Council Tax (they can send in the bailiffs); gas & electricity (they can cut you off); and water (though they cannot, at least in the UK).
    - Non-priority: less essential services, e.g. mobile phone, broadband, car loans; credit cards; everything else.
- Update the list regularly.
- Then make an income & expenditure budget based on your current spending pattern.
- Get it in perspective: analyse total debt relative to your total income, your discretionary income and your assets.
- Get help: there are lots of professionals who can help you.

"Cash can't buy you happiness but it comes attached to a better class of problem." – Woody Allen

Options

6

How can you get to where you want to be?

So you have invested time in reviewing your *Goal* and your current *Reality*. Now is the time to look at *Options*, in other words the ways in which you could bridge the gap.

The key question is: what possible ways can you think of that could move you from current *Reality* to your *Goal*? This is the time to do some thinking, before you make any decisions.

My favourite technique is this: at the top of an A4 pad (best of all, a yellow legal pad, as you guys on the other side of the Atlantic call them, and which I love dearly), write a very specific question.

For example: "how can I reduce my total debt to zero? (Or to £5,000? Or to three months' net income? Or to 20% of my net worth? Or whatever your goal is)…by such-and-such a date?"

Now force yourself to write *at least twenty* possible answers to that question, in one session. You could do this on your own, or with a partner or as a family: it is a kind of personal brainstorming session. If you have ever been involved in a brainstorming group through your work, you will remember that no evaluation is allowed at this stage. It's simply a technique for generating the maximum number of ideas. Although it is usually done in a group, this personal version of brainstorming can work well, in my experience. It's simply a way of accessing your creativity in order to solve your debt problem. (Who would have guessed that the words 'creativity' and 'debt' could be in the same sentence?)

If you are struggling to create the list, then that's where your coach or debt-counsellor might well go into 'mentor' mode and suggest some options that maybe didn't occur to you. After all, the stress of this situation is bound to inhibit clear thinking, so take all the help you can get; see 'Resources' for organisations that can help you.

So now you have a list of options. Some of your answers will be sensible and practical; others will seem to be off-the-wall. Some may be the opposite of others, and that does not matter. Writing the first five ideas will be easy; the next five may be a little harder. From number ten upwards might be a struggle. But sometimes when you arrive at number eighteen and you are about to give this up as a futile exercise, you dredge up a brilliant idea from the depths of your subconscious mind.

At this point, and especially if you don't have a real-life coach/counsellor/adviser, why not read the list to a friend?

Now, and only now, evaluate the ideas and decide – at least provisionally – which have the best chance of success AND which are concordant with your values. Then you can proceed to the all-important next step: action.

Choice is a wonderful thing, we are always told in this consumer society of ours; but too much choice can lead to confusion. However, in this situation I suggest you should look (sorry, could look; I am trying to cut 'should' from my vocabulary and maybe you could too) for three or more choices. As the saying goes, if you have two alternatives you have a dilemma; three or more represents real choice. If you have followed my suggestion to the letter, you will have 20 options, i.e. 20 choices; 20 *possible* ways of getting to your goal, out of which you can immediately reject several as unworkable and from which you'll choose one to guide your plan of action.

If you found that '20 ideas' exercise a struggle, here are a few questions that might help simplify your decision-making:

- Can you deal with the whole process yourself? If so, how? Could you…

- Pay it all, in instalments, and negotiate for time (in which case see Chapter 8)?
- Negotiate with your creditors for part-payment (see Chapter 10)?

• Or are you prepared to let someone else supervise your exit from debt? For example, would you consider…

- Filing for bankruptcy (see Chapter 9)?
- Signing up for another type of legally binding debt management plan (also Chapter 9)?

Right, you have defined your goal, evaluated your current reality and identified some *possible* ways of getting where you want to be. The options you have come up with probably fall within one of three groups, which I'll call Plan A, Plan B and Plan C, for the sake of simplicity.

Plan A – 'Pay It All'. Reduce your expenditure and/or increase your income so as to pay off 100% of your debts over an agreed period.

Plan B – 'Out Of Your Hands'. Either file for bankruptcy, or enter into a formal and binding debt management plan (or order), for example an IVA (Individual Voluntary Arrangement) in England, Wales and Northern Ireland. The nearest equivalent in Scotland is called a Protected Trust Deed. In Plan B, someone else – an officially appointed person – will have overall control of your finances for the duration of the plan or order, which could be from one to five years.

Plan C – 'Negotiate A Deal'. First, arrange a schedule to pay your priority debts in full. Then negotiate with your non-priority creditors to write off part of those debts in return for your agreement to pay the rest, either as a lump sum, if you can raise the funds, or in instalments.

These three types of solution are dealt with in more detail later, in Chapters 8, 9 and 10.

Plan A will involve you in making some tough choices about your budget and it will require you to negotiate with your creditors for more time to pay. Your degree of satisfaction will be massive if you can choose and implement a Plan A-type option, because you'll have paid back 100% of the debts. Read Chapter 8.

Plan B-type options would seem to be the mirror image of Plan A, as they involve solutions where your finances are supervised by someone else, not you, and the creditors will in general get the minimum return. It's worth talking about the psychological aspects of bankruptcy. We all have our attitudes to this and whether you want to file for bankruptcy as a way out of the situation will depend partly on the size of your debts; partly on what other options are open to you; partly on what assets you own that might be vulnerable in a bankruptcy; and last, but certainly not least, partly on your psychological reaction to the prospect of being bankrupt. For me, the bankruptcy option was one I resisted very much: however, since 1999 when I had to make that decision, it has become a more acceptable option, as both the stigma and the practical disadvantages have lessened greatly (again, at least in the UK). If you want to investigate this further, read Chapter 9 and then take professional advice.

As stated earlier, there are variations on bankruptcy, for example an IVA – an Individual Voluntary Arrangement (or a Protected Trust Deed in Scotland). An IVA is sometimes described as 'bankruptcy lite'. It does have many of the practical disadvantages of bankruptcy, and the period of supervision lasts longer, though it does not have the same perceived stigma. If you want to consider this route then, again, read Chapter 9 and take advice from an insolvency practitioner.

Plan C could be described as a compromise between A and B. If you want to consider a Plan C-type option, then read Chapter 10.

If you feel that you couldn't handle all this yourself unaided but Plan C is the way you want to go, then that's OK. When I was handling my own debt problem, the local Citizens Advice Bureau was happy to help me draft the letters. See the 'Resources' section at the end of the book for information on advice organisations and for my own letter templates.

Do not delay in developing your list of options; until you have taken this step you cannot make informed decisions. Delay in deciding can add thousands to your debts.

"Creditors have better memories than debtors." – Benjamin Franklin

Finally...

- There's free advice available, so use it.
- List your options; make the list as long as you can. If you have two options you have a dilemma; three or more, you have a choice. For instance:
  - Reduce spending? How?
  - Increase income? How?
  - Negotiate with your creditors?
  - File for bankruptcy?
  - Take out an IVA or equivalent?

"Days are lost lamenting over lost days. What you can do, or think you can do, begin it." – Goethe

Maximising Discretionary Income

7

A prerequisite of any debt management plan

I've usually found in the past that when my income increased, my spending increased. I also paid more tax, of course. Very soon, I forgot that I'd ever earned any less. I am sure this is a common experience.

However, you don't need more income in order to pay off some or all of those debts. You simply need more to be left over at the end of every week or month, after you've paid all your essential outgoings. That figure is called 'discretionary income' and it's the key to becoming debt-free.

Definitions

The Oxford English Dictionary defines that part of a person's income remaining after essential living costs as 'discretionary income'; however, you'll often find the term 'disposable income' used for the same purpose. Strictly speaking, though (again according to the OED), disposable income is simply gross income minus tax.

Although the two terms are nowadays used interchangeably – especially in the UK – for what we're discussing here, I prefer the term 'discretionary'. It's a good description because these are the funds over which you have 'discretion', i.e. you are the decision-maker. You, and no-one else, can decide how much of your discretionary income you'll spend on non-essentials and how much is available to pay down debt.

investopedia.com

This online dictionary says: "Discretionary income is the amount of an individual's income that is left for spending, investing or saving after taxes and personal necessities (such as food, shelter, and clothing) have been paid. Discretionary income includes money spent on luxury items, vacations and non-essential goods and services.

Discretionary income is derived from disposable income, which equals gross income minus taxes."

businessdictionary.com

Another online definition: "Discretionary income is the portion of an entity's income (did you know you were an entity?) available for saving, or spending on non-essentials. It is what remains after expenses for basics (such as food, clothing, shelter, utilities) and prior commitments (such as school fees and loans) are deducted from the disposable income."

This website adds, by the way, that the total amount of discretionary income in an economy is a key indicator of the level of possible economic growth and is the target of all commercial advertising.

From all the above you'll have gathered that I'm a bit of a nerd about defining things correctly. Otherwise we all have discussions that go nowhere. Alan Greenspan, the former Chairman of the Federal Reserve in the US, expressed it like this: "I know you think you understand what you thought I said but I'm not sure you realise that what you heard is not what I meant."

And if, like me, you found that statement unclear at first (which is probably what he intended), here's his much neater version of the same thing, which I love and for which he is probably most famous: "If I've made myself clear, you must have misunderstood me."

A banker with irony? We should have been warned.

Aids to calculation

If you have already had a debt advice session, you have probably been given an 'income and expenditure budget sheet', or words to that effect (sometimes called a 'Statement of Affairs', especially if it also includes space for your debts and your assets). That form will take you part of the way…but only part.

Those budget sheets or Statements of Affairs simply give you a snapshot of your current situation. If you are serious about becoming debt-free then you need more, i.e. you need to know your discretionary income. To calculate this important figure, you simply need the following data:

Pre-tax (i.e. gross) income
(whether from wage/salary, pensions, benefits or investments)
Minus income tax
Therefore net income after direct tax =
Minus National Insurance (UK) or equivalent:
Minus local taxes, e.g. Council Tax in Great Britain, rates in Northern Ireland:
Therefore "disposable" income =
Minus essential expenditure, as follows:
- Mortgage or rent:
- Essential utilities (water, gas, electricity; landline?):
- Food:
- Transport to & from work (include car standing costs only if car *essential* for work):
- Other essentials:
- Prior commitments (e.g. loan or card repayments; non-cancellable fees or memberships):

Total essential expenditure =
Therefore discretionary income =

There is a table ('Discretionary income table') in the Resources section, which you might find useful to copy and use.

That is just the start. The expenditure section of your income and expenditure statement is your budget as it is today. Whilst you are at it, why not add another column, which you will call your survival budget? In that one, you list only your essential outgoings. For example, 'if push comes to shove', could you/ would you reduce your expenditure on coffees, lunchtime sandwiches, and especially drinks? (booze, as you may know, provides only temporary relief from the stress you may feel about debt) Doing this survival budget could show you some alternatives.

So the term 'discretionary income' means that part of your income about which you can make decisions, for example how much of it will be spent and how much is available to pay off debt. To arrive at the figure, you'll deduct from your income those costs which cannot be avoided to provide the basics of life for you and your family: mortgage or rent, essential utilities (i.e. gas, electricity and water) and food, essential transport, unavoidable prior commitments.

You'll also subtract all taxes; both income tax, if it has not already been deducted at source, and local tax, e.g. council tax (if you live in Great Britain) or domestic rates (if you live in Northern Ireland). As we all know, "nothing is certain except death & taxes".

Discretionary income and paying off credit card debt

When you are working out your discretionary income from your spreadsheet and you come to the line marked 'prior commitments', I suggest that you include the minimum payments on your credit cards. How you will pay off the remaining balances is a later decision. By minimum I mean either the monthly minimum that the card agreement specifies; or even a lower figure, if you can't afford to pay the specified minimum and if you can negotiate a lower figure as a temporary measure.

Although you might not realise it, your credit card providers have a vested interest in keeping you from bankruptcy, because in that situation they'll recover very little. Thus it's in their interest to give you time to formulate a plan; and in the meantime they might well be prepared to freeze interest and penalty charges, that is, give you a moratorium. I say "might" but there is unfortunately no guarantee that they will. If you absolutely can't negotiate that moratorium, then set up direct debits to pay those minimum amounts (if you haven't already done so) on all your credit cards and store cards. Then you include only the monthly minimum payments for all your cards in the 'prior commitments' section of your spreadsheet.

If you can't make the monthly minimum and can't negotiate a lower figure or a moratorium, then do not despair. Making an offer of any kind of regular payment is better than nothing: it is evidence of goodwill on your part. It will be important if the matter ever ends up in court but let's not look on the dark side. A payment of even £1/month to each creditor might seem a waste of time but it seems to be an acceptable sign of good faith. And if you decide that that is the best you can do for now, then you just put the £1 payments into your discretionary income spreadsheet, whether or not the card provider has agreed.

Now, knowing your discretionary income, you can make your own decisions as to:

- How much you will use to pay off the balance of your card debts, and…
- How much you will spend on miscellaneous expenses.

Cutting spending

Maximizing discretionary income can, of course, be done by increasing income or reducing spending, or both. However, there's a strong reason for achieving this most important outcome by the spending route rather than the income route. It's usually possible to cut spending faster than one can find additional sources of income. The saying is that "expenditure cuts go straight to the bottom line" and in Chapter 8 I'll develop this. In Chapter 12 ('Keep up the good work') there are practical suggestions on cutting spending, some of which you might find worth considering.

Cutting spending with the Spendometer

In the battle to control spending, here's an idea for those of you who prefer technology rather than paper spreadsheets or even back-of-envelope calculations. If you have an iPhone or similar type of mobile phone, there is a neat little tool called a Moneybasics Spendometer that provides a fun way of tracking your spending. If you have a device like this that helps you track spending on a frequent basis, you're more likely to be able to reduce it.

The Spendometer is provided by Credit Action (now called The Money Charity) and it works on any mobile that can access the web. The application is provided free both to download and to use, although they say: "on some mobile phone networks you might pay a small amount for the download." See 'Resources' for the link.

"It is very iniquitous to make me pay my debts – you have no idea of the pain it gives one." – Byron

Finally…

- Discretionary income is that part of your income that's left after taxes and *essential* expenditure.
- In order to pay off debt, it is necessary to maximise discretionary income.
- You might decide it is possible to increase discretionary income by finding new income sources. However it is generally faster and easier to achieve what you want by cutting spending.
- That might involve a rethink of what you previously thought of as essential spending. "Do I need this or just want it?"

"Money is better than poverty, if only for financial reasons." – Woody Allen

Plan A
Pay it All

8

Could you do so? How soon?

Do you think it will be possible to pay off all your debts in a reasonable time, i.e. within a period that your creditors would accept?

I may have said this before but it's worth repeating: your personal debt recovery plan is a project for your home office, or your kitchen or dining-table, where you can spread out all the papers you need. It'd be a good idea to get a lever-arch file, or similar, for all related correspondence while you're dealing with your debts. Because, even if you believe you *can* pay it all, it'll take time. Negotiating for that extra time will need correspondence.

So you want to find a way of gradually eliminating 100% of your debts, e.g. by reducing your expenditure, increasing your income, cashing in some assets such as pension funds (if you're old enough), insurance policies, that piano you never play, etc, over a specific period. Is that period realistic for you and acceptable to your creditors? The main issues are whether those creditors will give you the time you need and – very important, this – whether they are prepared to freeze interest and other charges while you are repaying. There's only one way to find out: ask them. You may be surprised at how flexible many lenders and other creditors can be, especially if they fear that you might otherwise file for bankruptcy, in which case they'd probably get almost nothing. Gently hinting that bankruptcy is an option you are considering might motivate them in the right direction.

Who is going to do the negotiation? At the end of the day the buck stops with you, of course, but you are not alone. Depending on where you live, you may be able to get free help from an advice charity or from an insolvency practitioner. If not, do you have any supporters who can help? Do you have friends who have relevant skills, contacts or experience?

You have evaluated your current reality in financial terms. You have reviewed the options for getting to where you want to be. Is it feasible to 'pay it all'? Right now, it might seem very unlikely that that you can pay all that you owe within a reasonable time. It might even be the case that you have a problem in covering the monthly minimum payments on your credit cards, let alone the full balance, and therefore the amount owing is increasing every month. If that's the case then you are probably receiving lots of payment demands; those demands add to the stress of an already stressful situation and therefore you may well think it's unlikely you could 'pay it all.' However, you might be surprised at what can be achieved simply by communicating with your creditors.

Communication

As mentioned in the previous chapter, it could be that if you inform your creditors that you are in difficulties, they will give you time to put a plan together. It might also be that they will agree to freeze interest charges – and also freeze penalty charges for missed payments – while you are putting that plan together. Because many people who are in debt try to keep the matter secret, for quite understandable reasons, they do not 'come clean' to their creditors until it is too late – even though those same creditors may well have realised that there are problems. In the short term the card companies, for example, might be happy to collect the interest if you only pay the minimum every month (i.e. you are 'a revolver', in their jargon) but in the long term they would be saddled with a bad debt if you should be forced into bankruptcy. So they have a vested interest in helping you to solve the problem by giving you time…provided, and only provided, you discuss it with them.

So the first step is to buy time by making your creditors aware you have a problem and telling them that you want to find a way to pay in full. In Chapter 2, I made a case for carrying out any negotiations with creditors in writing, rather than on the phone. So this process will require you to send some letters (maybe a lot of letters, depending on how many creditors you have) and you'll find templates for those among the resources at the end of this book.

The next step, of course, is to formulate a plan. That plan will be based on analysing your financial situation in detail; finding out if there is a better way of allocating existing funds so as to speed up the process of reducing your debt; and then maybe finding ways to increase your income and/or decrease your expenditure. If, however, after serious consideration, you are really convinced that you can do none of those things, then Plan A is not a realistic option for you and you need to move on to Chapter 9 or 10.

Discretionary income: the source of debt payback

In the last chapter I discussed how to calculate discretionary income (again, refer to the table in Resources to help you calculate your own). If you now know what that figure is, you can make your own decisions as to how much you will spend and how much you can afford to use monthly to pay down your debt.

In the UK, most unsecured personal debt is on credit cards, so getting your strategy right in this area is crucial. If possible, allocate as much as you can of your payback funds to the card bearing the highest interest rate. This will probably be a store card, if you have any. When you've paid that one off, repeat the process with the card bearing the second-highest interest rate, and so on. It sounds too simple to be true; but you probably know that there can be large variations in card interest rates.

A more sophisticated method is the 'snowball' tool, which is described later in this chapter.

Doing this will minimise your overall interest bill and thus increase the speed at which you can 'pay it all'; it is a flexibility which is generally denied to you if you follow Plan B or Plan C, where you will need to offer all your creditors the same 'dividend', expressed as pence in the pound or as a percentage of the debt.

Increasing income vs reducing expenditure

So far we've talked about a possible reallocation of your funds, so that payback could be accelerated even within your current financial situation by paying off different cards at different rates. Could you improve that situation further by increasing income or by reducing expenditure?

Only you can possibly know if there is any way to increase your income, whether it is though overtime working; finding an extra part-time job; claiming benefits you are entitled to but didn't claim before; or turning a hobby into a spare-time business. The options are different for everyone on the planet, so you could conduct a personal brainstorming session of the kind I described in Chapter 6.

Short-term solutions

Are you sure you are maximising the net income you get from your existing sources? First of all, are you paying too much tax? If you are an employee, on someone else's payroll, then the number of allowances you can claim are limited. However, if you are self-employed then I am sure you will know that options are wide, either to reduce the tax you will pay next time or to reduce your current liability if you are overdue on this year's or previous years' payments.

Also on the income side: are you entitled to benefits of any kind? The media love to run stories about benefit fraud but the other side of the coin is that benefits are under-claimed, in the UK alone, not by millions but by billions of pounds every year. The figure is between £4 and 7 billion (between $6 and $10.5 billion) per annum, according to a report by the London School of Economics. That's partly because of pride but mostly because people are not aware of their entitlements. If you think this might be you, consult your local debt advice centre.

Emergency help from charities

Grants are available from a variety of charitable organisations. In the UK, for example, the Royal British Legion is a useful source of help for ex-service personnel who find themselves with debt problems. Their website states: "About 9.5 million people in the UK are eligible for our support." Those eligibility criteria are very generous: you only have to have served in the forces for a minimum of seven days to qualify. Dependants of anyone who has served are also eligible. If you fit into one of these categories, the Legion's 'Immediate Needs Scheme' is worth checking out.

Tax credits

Charity help is an under-used resource and the same is true of tax credits. The UK system has often been accused of being over-complicated; I have no personal experience of the system but I can well believe those accusations. At the risk of repetition…get advice. For example, Citizens Advice has a useful little booklet called 'Help yourself…to get more money', which deals with this.

Radical approaches

Alternatively – or as well as the above – you could try a different approach, as described in the chapter on 'portfolio working' in Charles Handy's book 'The Age of Unreason.'

Handy recommends that as we go through life, and certainly by the time we have reached middle age (whatever that means for you), we develop a 'portfolio' of skills and talents that we could supply to a variety of clients, if we choose. Some of those services might well be unpaid, but no matter. He says we should not distinguish between paid and unpaid work: "it's all work." Handy tells the story of an English acquaintance, a 48-year-old senior account director for a large advertising agency. He had been told by the Chairman that they "felt he should move on". The company had made him a generous termination offer but now he needed a new job. "What are you good at?" asked Handy. "Running an account group in an advertising agency", came the reply.

"Why don't you try this", said Handy, "…contact twenty people who know you well, at work or outside work, and ask them to name just one thing that you do well, in their experience of you."

The friend, being in Handy's words a somewhat reticent Englishman (a reticent guy working in advertising?), found it difficult but in a couple of weeks he came back with that list of twenty things. He found the list surprising, partly because none of the friends had mentioned running an account group, the only thing he thought he did well. There were ideas for business ventures, voluntary activities, teaching, personal learning, writing, and so on. None of them added up to what he called a proper job.

The friend went back to advertising, not as an account director but as a director in charge of administration for a smaller agency. It was 'a proper job'. Handy says, "I lost that one but I suspect he'll be back in a year or two, when he realises that one full-time job in advertising is not the only way, or even the best way, to use his many and varied talents."

Portfolio people

I love the term 'portfolio working', which is described as 'a lifestyle in which the individual holds a number of jobs, clients and types of work', all at the same time. For examples, look no further than the originator of the term, Charles Handy himself. The Anglo-Irish economist and best-selling author began his career with Shell Petroleum (a background he shares with the UK's Business Secretary Vince Cable, though the latter spent rather more time there) and then the engineering group Charter Consolidated (now Charter International) before diversifying his activities and living the freelance life. He was subsequently co-founder and Professor of the London Business School.

He is quoted as saying, "I told my children when they were leaving education that they would be well advised to look for customers, not bosses."

To gauge Handy's style these days, as a portfolio person, read the first few lines of his autobiography:

> Some years ago I was helping my wife arrange an exhibit of her photographs when I was approached by a man who had been looking at the pictures. "I hear that Charles Handy is here," he said. "Indeed he is," I replied, "and I am he." He looked at me rather dubiously for a moment, and then said, "Are you sure?" It was, I told him, a good question because over time there had been many versions of Charles Handy…not all of which I was particularly proud of.

That remark seems typical of the self-effacing nature of the man because, if there is such a thing as a philosopher of management and organisational behaviour, then it is he. Handy has been rated among 'the Thinkers 50', a list of the most influential living management thinkers in the world; in 2001 he was second on that list.

Looking eastwards, two examples from the first half of the twentieth century have just been brought to my attention by a radio programme. Russian composer Borodin (symphonies, string quartets and the opera Prince Igor, which was famously 'sampled', to use modern jargon, for the musical Kismet) was also a successful and celebrated research chemist (I probably learned that many years ago but had forgotten it). He is credited with the discovery of the Aldol reaction (which I do vaguely remember learning about); moreover the reaction known in the West as the Hunsdiecker reaction was called the Borodin reaction in the former Soviet Union. Not satisfied with that, he was also a writer and poet 'in his spare time', whatever that phrase means.

And what about the internationally celebrated pianist and composer Paderewski? His portfolio included being Prime Minister of the Polish Republic. A BBC Radio 3 announcer described him as "the ultimate moonlighting musician"; I prefer to think of him as the pre-eminent Polish portfolio person.

And that reminded me: while we are on the subject of

moonlighting musicians, have you heard of the violinist Einstein? Yes, that'll be Albert Einstein himself. He who said that imagination is more important than knowledge, which shows immediately that he was a portfolio person. Apparently it wasn't enough to have been the physicist, philosopher and author who is widely regarded as one of the most influential and best-known scientists and intellectuals of all time, often regarded as the father of modern physics. As well as all that, he was a concert-level violinist. As Jack Black (the author, not the film actor) says, "If he had concentrated on the violin, you would still have heard of him".

'Moonlighting musician' would also be a perfect description for William Herschel, the polymath who is known mostly as an astronomer. He discovered Uranus and two of its major moons…not to mention composing twenty-four symphonies and lots of other music (Moon? Music? Apologies for my corny link; I couldn't resist it). By the way, I love the fact he is known (in the UK, anyway) as a British astronomer, although he was born in Hannover to German parents. Why? He moved here! He was clearly a forerunner of the current system in many sports, where top performers change national allegiance by changing residence.

And finally, also on our shores: the author Sir Arthur Conan Doyle was most famous for his fictional creation, Sherlock Holmes. Maybe you knew that he was also a GP (that's what a family doctor is called in the UK); but did you know that he was also goalkeeper for Portsmouth Association Football Club? That was the predecessor of Portsmouth FC, the largest fan-owned club in England. 'Pompey', as it's affectionately known, has had a disappointing time on and off the pitch in recent seasons; relegated from the Premiership having also accumulated massive debts. So Conan Doyle was a true portfolio man. What a pity that Sherlock Holmes was not still around to solve the football club's problems.

What's 'the moral of the story'? All those stories, in fact, from Charles Handy to Conan Doyle? Maybe we could take inspiration from them, by thinking about our many talents (we all have them, even if they have been underused) and pinpointing which of them have the potential to bring in some extra money.

Reducing expenditure

However much you may wish to increase your income, major changes cannot, in general, be made overnight. Particularly in the economic situation we're in at the time of writing, that part-time job might involve extra travel costs; that small business start-up will require some investment. It could be a long-drawn-out process to find the opportunity that suits you; once found, that extra work requires more of your waking hours, and time is a limited resource. You'll also be paying more tax. Those downsides are true even if the extra income you seek is in a field in which you are already working. If you choose to try – or are forced to try, due to circumstances – a new field, with or without the Charles Handy 'portfolio' approach, it will take even longer.

On the other hand, decreasing expenditure is something that almost everyone could consider. The effects are immediate and, to use an old business saying, "expenditure cuts go straight to the bottom line". In other words, the amount you save is immediately available, in full, to start paying off those debts.

The depressed state of the economy at the time of writing, both in the UK and almost everywhere else, is a reason why finding additional income is hard. However, every cloud has a silver lining and this silver lining is that today it's a buyer's market for most things. I have never seen so many 'special offers' in my life. Ignore the official inflation figures you read in the press; you can reduce your personal inflation figure to below zero…but only if you are more ruthless with yourself in distinguishing what you need from what you want, and if you become better at finding the best deals for the necessities of life.

If you carry out this exercise honestly, you might well be amazed at the difference between your 'survival budget' and your current spending pattern. For more on the subject of reducing spending see Chapter 12 of this book ('Keep up the good work'), because the principles of how to free up the maximum amount of cash to 'Pay It All' are exactly the same as those that'll keep you out of debt in the future.

Don't keep rainy day money

Do you have any savings? You might answer: "are you crazy? I've used them up long ago." However, many people who are facing severe debt problems, and are 'maxed out' on their credit cards, turn out to have money squirreled away in another account, 'for a rainy day' (I was one of them). Well, as this is a rainy day, (and right now you are earning very little interest on those savings) it makes no sense to hold on to savings at the same time as you have unsustainable debts.

That statement is not original. In 2007, an article in the money pages of the Daily Telegraph concluded with this simple phrase, with which I found it hard to argue but hadn't realised before. "Paying down debt remains the best risk-free, tax-free investment in town." I love that statement; I suspect it is always true.

Dealing with priority debts: mortgage arrears

If you are in mortgage arrears then your first priority must be to find a way to clear them. If not, your lender can take legal action to have you evicted.

However, if the lender knows that you are making a serious effort to sort out your debts, they might allow you more time. Once more, the key is early communication: don't sweep the problem under the mat.

Reducing your costs

There are several options for cutting down your mortgage costs. Depending on the type of mortgage, you might be able to:

- Switch from repayment to interest-only mortgage.
- Increase the term.

- Reduce your monthly interest payments.
- Shop around for a cheaper deal with another lender. However, you may have to pay charges for the switch and you'll still have to pay off the arrears.

Sadly, none of these is entirely pain-free. Solving the short-term problem could either involve fees, in the case of changing lender, or it could increase your interest payments long-term. Consult an independent financial adviser first if you are thinking of taking any of these steps and, once again, consult the lender. They may be able to help; but only if you get in touch with them.

Paying off arrears

Before you do discuss paying off the arrears, first work out your discretionary income; see elsewhere in this book for how to do that.

You will also need to decide how to pay off those arrears. You may have several options for doing this:

- Pay extra towards the arrears each month on top of your regular payments.
- Have the arrears added to your capital and paid back over the remaining term; this will, of course, increase your overall interest costs.
- Give up your endowment policy, if you still have one, or sell it to an investor, and use the lump sum towards your arrears; however, you will need to find another way to pay off the capital and you might also need to find alternative life insurance cover, so consult a financial adviser first.

Dealing with your lender

Once you have worked out a way of dealing with your mortgage arrears, write to your lender and set out your offer. Is it one that you can keep to and will it clear the arrears within the period of the mortgage? Include a financial statement showing how you have worked out the offer. If the lender resists at first, stress that an affordable offer is in both of your interests, because you are more likely to keep to it.

Start to make regular payments against the arrears, even small ones. Even if your lender doesn't accept the offer, it may help your case if you are ever taken to court.

If you haven't been able to reach agreement on how to pay off your arrears, they will probably take you to court and try and get possession. However, the good news (if there is any good news in all this) is that, before they take you to court, they have to follow a fixed procedure called a protocol. This involves their taking a number of steps, such as discussing the reason for the arrears with you and giving you notice that they will start legal action if you have broken a payment agreement.

If you do go to court, the judge may allow you to stay in your property as long as you keep to an agreement to pay. The judge will take into account whether the mortgage lender followed the protocol. If you are in this situation, get help from an adviser.

If you can't pay your arrears

If you aren't able to clear your arrears, a court will probably give your lender permission to evict you from your home and your lender will sell the property. If they don't make enough from the sale to cover the money you owe on your mortgage, you will have to pay the difference, which is called a shortfall.

If you can't find any other way of clearing your arrears, it might be better to try and sell the property yourself, rather than wait to get evicted and let your mortgage lender sell it. This is because they are likely to get a lot less for it than you would, leaving you with a debt to pay. Properties which have been repossessed often sell for a lot less. Also, lenders often sell at auctions where sale prices tend to be lower.

Selling the property yourself and downsizing, or renting for a period, would give you a lump sum which you could use to pay off your mortgage; if you have enough left over, you may even be able to use it to pay off other debts.

Another option you may want to think about is a mortgage rescue scheme. These schemes are also known as buy back, sale and rent back or a sale and lease back scheme. These are schemes which offer to buy your property and rent it back to you. However, be very careful about signing up to a mortgage rescue scheme run by a private company. Not all these schemes are trustworthy and some companies will buy at below the market value. Schemes run by local authorities or housing associations are generally better, but there aren't many of these.

Don't be tempted to just leave the property and hand back the keys to your mortgage lender unless you've sold the property or there is a court order to evict you. You won't gain anything because you will still be responsible for mortgage payments and buildings insurance until the property is sold, and will still have to make up any shortfall if the sale doesn't make enough to cover what you owe.

If your lender asks you to give up the keys, you don't have to do so unless they have a court order.

Note

This section on mortgage arrears has been based on an extract from the Citizens Advice (UK) organisation's 'Adviceguide' website. Readers who are in mortgage arrears are advised to check that site for any changes to protocols.

Dealing with priority debts: rent arrears

This is also a priority debt, for the obvious reason that you could, in the worst case, lose your home.

The situation varies according to whether you rent from a private landlord, from your local council or from a housing association. Because of that complication, all I'll say is this: if in rent arrears, communicate with your landlord and consult an adviser before the problem gets worse.

Reacquainting yourself with the reality of cash

I am indebted to *The Times* and journalist Jane Shilling for that headline about reacquainting with the reality of cash. In other words, you are more likely to keep an eye on your spending if you go back to the good old-fashioned method of paying for stuff with cash.

You could put all your regular (and essential!) commitments on Direct Debit; then decide how much 'housekeeping allowance' you are going to give yourself. Draw that amount in cash on the same day every week, and don't draw more, and leave your cards at home (unless you are travelling and need one for emergencies) and don't go over your cash limit. Then your spending will seem more real.

To begin, it'll be hard. You'll often reach the end of the money before the end of the week; but when you've got into the habit of thrift, you might be pleasantly surprised how satisfying it is to get to the end of the week and find you've some cash left. Jane Shilling of *The Times* says:

> Having worked out a budget, the first thing I did was to reacquaint myself with the reality of cash. It felt a curiously archaic thing to do. Cards are easy, cards are safe(ish). The trouble is, that cards don't really feel like spending. Hand it over, tap in the PIN, here come the goods and somehow I have no sensation of having spent any actual money at all.

Credit card debt: the 'snowball' way to pay

Elsewhere in this book I talk about paying off non-priority debts on a pro rata basis. In fact in many situations you will have little choice. If you decide to go for 'Plan C', and you need to persuade your creditors to forgive part of your debts, then pro rata is the way to go, i.e. they all get the same dividend; the same number of pence in the pound, or cents on the dollar or euro. No creditor likes to feel that another creditor is getting a better deal.

However, if you are trying to 'Pay it all', then it would be useful to know in which order to pay off the credit cards. Elsewhere I mention paying the ones with the highest interest rate first, and that is just common sense. A more sophisticated approach can be found via a little online tool called the 'snowball debt calculator', which can be found via the MoneySavingExpert website. You can enter the details of your card debts (up to 20 of them) and it makes the calculation for you. You can find it at: http://www.whatsthecost.com/snowball.aspx

Ruthlessness with cards

How ruthless are you prepared to be? Why not cut up all your cards, except one credit card (the one with the lowest interest rate) for major emergencies and your debit card for minor emergencies. But try to leave even those two at home on days when your schedule is predictable, e.g. from home to work and back home again. That way you are removing yourself from temptation and you become more aware of your spending patterns.

Negotiations and the 'broken record' technique

Here's something worth remembering, whatever you are negotiating for.

When negotiating with creditors for more time to pay or even just a little time to come up with a plan, (or anything else), you can use the 'broken record' technique when necessary. The name comes from the glory days of vinyl – and previously shellac – records, when the occasional crack would cause interesting and repetitive sound-effects.

If the creditor's response appears to ignore something you've said, simply repeat what you said in your previous letter. Many people (and companies) don't really read or take notice of things the first time (intentionally or unintentionally; it doesn't matter which). So if you don't get the response you want, just repeat yourself in the next letter, and so on ad infinitum.

Cast studies

Mrs Johnson

One of the first clients I saw as a volunteer CAB adviser comes to mind some 9 years ago. At the time of her first visit she had approximately £35,000 worth ($52,500) of consumer credit debt owed to around 15 different creditors.

She worked in the finance industry and her terms of employment strictly prohibited being in unmanageable debt. Her problems began with a relatively small change of circumstances which affected her income and she moved from a position of managing credit to financial difficulty. She found herself unable to meet her commitments on existing credit and began further borrowing to keep up minimum payments in the hope that her circumstances would improve. An inevitable spiral of debt followed reaching the point where cash simply ran out.

The client's greatest worry was that interest and charges would run out of control and her employers would eventually become aware of her insolvency.

We agreed to write to the creditors distributing available income on a fair basis after essential expenses and asked for all charges and interest to be frozen. After protracted negotiations, agreements were reached with all the companies concerned. We recently learned that the client has paid all the accounts in full and is completely debt-free.

Christine Stanton

Christine Stanton had debts totalling £40,000 ($60,000) and an annual income of £19,000 ($28,500); she was advised to declare herself bankrupt. She rejected that advice and five years later she was totally debt-free. She was interviewed widely, in both the print media and online financial discussion boards, where she said she'd got out of debt by "hard work, sacrifice and scrimping". She also said that she'd "got herself into the mess"; therefore it was her "moral obligation" to get out of it.

Christine's borrowing began with student loans. But she

became pregnant before graduating, so she was forced to drop out of education in order to work and support herself as a single mother. Her income, however, was not enough to cover basic living expenses. Thus she began to borrow on credit cards and ran up an overdraft; the debts started to increase.

Childcare was a major cost; to pay for it, Christine added loans to her credit card debts. Four years later her minimum monthly repayments had soared to over £1,100 ($1,650). Then, to make matters even worse, her son's father, who had been helping financially, died unexpectedly.

Eventually she sought help from her local CAB (Citizens Advice Bureau), because she was at her wits' end and couldn't meet her commitments. They suggested she went on to benefits but she rejected that advice. It was then suggested that Christine enter into a plan controlled by a debt management company but she felt that the fees would use up too much of the money she wanted to use to repay her debts. She decided instead to handle it herself.

What to do? "I sat and wrote everything down," says Christine. "All the debts; all the outgoings; all the income. Then I cried."

But she didn't cry for long. She approached her creditors one by one with the reality of her situation and told them how much she would repay on a regular basis.

She drew up a schedule of essential expenses and cut out everything else. She shopped around for a cheaper energy supplier. She cancelled her gym membership. She kept her food bills low by doing her supermarket shopping late on Saturdays to get the bargains.

She needed internet access for work but it had an unexpected bonus, as it became a key source of support. In particular, the Motley Fool website (www.fool.co.uk) led her to an online community of people sharing tips on debt management; it also provided emotional support when nasty letters from the bank arrived. That bank (which had lent her a fair chunk of the debt) told her they didn't want her banking with them any more and demanded that she repay her overdraft immediately. In response, Christine made a proposal to pay off the overdraft in instalments; after extensive correspondence, the bank finally agreed.

Christine says that she couldn't have survived without the support of the online community. She found lots of people in the same boat and the messages they exchanged lifted her spirits.

Christine also discovered, or maybe rediscovered, her entrepreneurial streak. First, she started to buy second-hand clothes to resell on eBay. Later, she had the idea of moving into a larger rental property which allowed her, with the co-operation of the landlord, to sublet rooms to overseas students. She would make huge batches of cheap but wholesome foods, such as pasta and chilli sauces, to provide meals for the students. Although she paid a higher rent and council tax than she had before, she still made hundreds of pounds profit per month from the rent the students paid, which contributed greatly to her debt repayments. Over two years, the profits from these rents enabled Christine to reduce her indebtedness by £10,000 ($15,000).

Christine couldn't afford expensive days out with her son; however, on fine days they'd take sandwiches to the park and play football. She says that what he gained from the experience is that he has grown up knowing the value of money. "He loves the outdoors but he also knows what compound interest is."

In addition, Christine had to rethink her work situation: David had moved up to secondary school and her employer's business was not large enough to be able to offer flexible working hours. So her goal now is to start her own business, so that she can work around school hours. She also wants to buy a house eventually. She knows it won't be easy, because house prices in her area are high; however, being debt-free has made her feel she can cope with anything.

After those five years, during which almost all her discretionary income went to pay off creditors, making the last payment was a wonderful moment. Christine says it had been "a pleasant surprise to discover you can live without spending quite so much money."

Christine summarises her advice to those in the same situation, as follows:

- "Do write it down."
- "Cut back on the things you don't need."
- "Reduce your outgoings."
- "Use credit cards cleverly (with zero % interest)."
- "Stay on top of things."
- "It's not the end of the world. It's only money."

Jack Jameson

Mr Jameson is self-employed; he borrowed £10,500 ($15,750) from a major high street bank for work on an asset that was essential to his business. Although he said he didn't want it, he found himself committed to Payment Protection Insurance at an extra cost of £2,694 ($4,041). When he realised this had happened, he tried to get the bank to cancel it but they told him it was past the 'cooling-off period'. After having had no success in getting the matter sorted out, he wrote to a national newspaper, who told him what he suspected: that the cost of this Payment Protection Insurance (PPI) was unreasonably high.

The chance of a successful PPI claim was low for Mr Jameson, because he was self-employed, therefore could not be sacked. The bank knew this when it persuaded him to take the insurance, but they claimed he also had valuable sickness and accident cover; they had dug their heels in and would not concede that the policy had been mis-sold. After the newspaper's intervention, the bank agreed to refund all the remaining premiums (£2,023/$3,035, plus interest) as a gesture of goodwill; thus Mr Jameson will pay off his loan seven months early. The moral of this case is this: writing to a newspaper's money pages is often worthwhile.

"A bank is a place that will lend you money if you can prove that you don't need it."– Bob Hope

Finally...

- At an early stage, let your bank and all your creditors know about your problems. They might be able to help.
- Deal first with priority debts, e.g. any arrears in mortgage, rent, Council Tax (GB: domestic rates in NI) and essential utilities; and any debts that could, in the worst case, deprive you of your liberty.
- Reply to all demands in writing: promptly, politely, professionally, setting out your situation and (if you know) what you propose to do or what you need from them (e.g. more info, more time, interest freeze, etc). Keep copies of all correspondence and be persistent if they don't agree at first.
- If anyone offers to lend you more money, e.g. through a debt-consolidation loan, take independent advice before proceeding. If you do decide to go for such a loan, resist any demand to secure it against your home.
- There's free advice available, so use it. An advice organisation's support and procedures add legitimacy while negotiating for more time to pay. It's an example of 'negotiating with limited authority.'
- Creditors might agree to freeze interest charges while you sort things out. Meanwhile make an offer of some sort: even £1/month shows willing.
- You might want to give a higher priority to debts to small businesses, or friends, over debts to major banks or credit card companies. If you go for Plan A that possibility might well be open to you; but not if you go for Plans B or C.
- Ask yourself: "If push came to shove, what could I do without?" How little could you live on, if everything depended on it? The more effectively you answer those questions, the faster you can 'pay it all.'
- Reacquaint yourself with the realities of cash: put regular commitments on Direct Debit, review your discretionary

income, give yourself a spending money budget. Now draw it in cash weekly and stick to it, minimising the use of cards.

"I don't like money, actually, but it quiets my nerves." – Joe Louis

Plan B
Out of your Hands

9

Bankruptcy & other legally-binding debt management plans

If your debt problem is severe, and you think Plan A is out of the question, then you may wish to consider bankruptcy or an Individual Voluntary Arrangement (IVA), or some other solution where both the negotiation of the plan and its subsequent management are taken out of your hands. Moreover, your financial affairs will be supervised for a period of between one and five years. These are what I call Plan B solutions.

Whether Plan B is right for you will, of course, depend on your own particular circumstances. This book cannot tell you; it cannot make that decision for you; no book can. Therefore, before considering this option, or variants of this option, take advice about your situation. See the end of this chapter for guidance on finding the right professional to advise you.

Bankruptcy

Bankruptcy is an option that cannot be taken lightly. If you are thinking of making yourself bankrupt, seek specialist insolvency advice first.

Many organisations offer insolvency advice and debt counselling: most are entirely reputable and offer a professional service. However, according to the UK Government's Insolvency Service, "others are controlled by individuals with no obvious qualifications who appear to be motivated mainly by a desire to exploit an already difficult situation. Beware, particularly, of unsolicited approaches through the post or by telephone."

Insolvency practitioners are the specialists in this area; at the end of this chapter you'll find a checklist of questions you can ask to find the right one for your circumstances.

Bankruptcy is a serious matter. You will have to give up possessions of value and, very likely, your interest in your home. If you run a business, you may have to close it.

There are, however, alternatives to bankruptcy. Evaluate these alternatives, as they might be more suitable in your situation.

Bankruptcy's main benefit, according to the Insolvency Service, is that it will free you from overwhelming debts so that you can make a fresh start, subject to some restrictions; meanwhile your assets will be shared out fairly among your creditors.

Anyone can go bankrupt, including individual members of a business partnership. There are separate procedures for dealing with companies and for partnerships but I am focussing on individual, not corporate, bankruptcy in this section. You as an individual can be made bankrupt by a court making a bankruptcy order, which it can do only after a 'bankruptcy petition' has been presented; either by you yourself or by one or more of your creditors, provided that any such creditor is owed at least £750 ($1,125) by you and the debt is unsecured.

After the bankruptcy order is made, your case will be dealt with either by the official receiver, who is an officer of the court, or by an insolvency practitioner, who is a professional specialising in such work and appointed by the court. One of these two will become your 'trustee' and will be responsible for disposing of your assets and making payments to your creditors.

When you are bankrupt you do not, in general, make payments to your creditors; they make a claim to your trustee instead. There are, however, a few exceptions, payment for which you remain responsible. For example:

- Secured creditors (e.g. any mortgage you may have).
- 'Non-provable' debts (e.g. court fines and maintenance arrears under divorce settlements).
- Student loans.

Although debts that you owe at the time you are made bankrupt will be dealt with by your trustee, you yourself must then pay continuing commitments, such as mortgage or rent, utilities etc.

The trustee will tell the creditors how much money is to be shared out; then the creditors make formal claims. The costs of the bankruptcy process, including the trustee's fees, are paid first from the money available, although you will have to fund the costs of your application and a deposit for costs. Those costs are substantial; a fact that seems somewhat strange, as the process is designed to provide a solution for people in financial difficulties and their creditors.

The whole process can become very public, because your trustee may place newspaper advertisements, inviting creditors to submit claims. If it takes some time to deal with assets these advertisements could appear over a considerable period.

Your home

Here is the most significant downside of a bankruptcy. If you own your home (whether or not it is mortgaged), your interest in it (i.e. your equity) becomes part of the 'estate'. Therefore your home might well have to be sold.

However, if your husband, wife or children are living with you, it might be possible to put off the sale for up to a year, while you find alternative accommodation.

If it takes some time for the trustee to sell your home; and if in the meantime you are discharged from bankruptcy (see below), you may still lose the value of your interest in the home. This area is complicated, so you – and any other interested party, e.g. your partner – should take advice as a matter of urgency if you own your home.

Other assets

The trustee, before disposing of your assets, will let you keep certain items, particularly any you need for work (e.g. tools, vehicles) and those you and your family need in the home (e.g. furniture, clothing, bedding, household equipment etc). Then the trustee takes control of all other assets.

Pensions

According to the Insolvency Service, any private pension fund you have built up cannot generally be claimed as an asset if the bankruptcy petition was presented on or after 29 May 2000, as long as the scheme was approved by HM Revenue & Customs.

For petitions presented before then, trustees could claim some types of pensions. That is the situation I personally was in, back in 1999; therefore, one of the main reasons why I did not opt for bankruptcy would not generally apply today.

Payments from your income

Your trustee may apply for an Income Payment Order (IPO), requiring you to make contributions from your income. However, an order will not be made if you would not be left with sufficient income to meet the 'reasonable domestic needs' of you and your family. IPOs continue for up to 3 years and may well continue after you have been discharged from bankruptcy, but can be changed if there is an increase – or decrease – in your income.

Restrictions during bankruptcy

Your credit record will, of course, be affected by bankruptcy.

- You cannot obtain credit of £500 ($750) or more without disclosing the fact you are bankrupt.
- You cannot carry on business in a different name from that in which you were made bankrupt, without telling all those concerned the name in which you were made bankrupt (and of course you have to close down the existing business).
- You cannot be involved, even indirectly, in forming, managing or promoting a limited company, or acting as company director, without the court's permission.
- You may not hold certain public offices or become a trustee of a charity or a pension fund.
- There are also restrictions on how you may operate

a bank account. You may open a new account but must inform the bank you are bankrupt, and you must not obtain overdraft facilities without informing them.

Discharge from bankruptcy

The period before discharge from bankruptcy has been shortened considerably in recent times. If you were made bankrupt on or after 1 April 2004, you will be automatically discharged, i.e. freed from restrictions, after a maximum of 12 months; it could even be less, if the trustee's enquiries are concluded quickly. Discharge releases you from most of the debts you owed at the time of the bankruptcy order.

After you have been discharged you can borrow money, carry on business etc, without the bankruptcy restrictions. However, some assets you owned at the time of your bankruptcy (e.g. your home, if it has not been sold) will not revert to you. With some of these assets your spouse, a partner, a relative or friend may want to buy your interest and can negotiate with the trustee to do so.

Alternatives to Bankruptcy

Individual Voluntary Arrangements (IVAs)

An Individual Voluntary Arrangement or IVA is a widely-used and, for many debtors, more acceptable alternative to bankruptcy. It is a formal procedure under the Insolvency Act 1986 which, like bankruptcy, deals with all your creditors together. Also as with bankruptcy, a proportion of your debts will be written off.

An IVA can be taken out by anyone in England, Wales or Northern Ireland with unaffordable unsecured debts and a stable income to allow a scheme of repayments. The nearest equivalent in Scotland is called a Protected Trust Deed.

An IVA is a legally-binding agreement. An Insolvency Practitioner (IP) will assist you in preparing a proposal to present to your creditors, in which they will all receive the same 'dividend' expressed as pence in the pound.

The practitioner's report on your affairs will assist the creditors to accept the offer. A condition of an IVA is that the offer has to be accepted by 75% of creditors in value terms; however this provision could exclude smaller creditors. If accepted by 75%, then it is binding on all creditors, even those that did not accept. Your IP will attempt to gain acceptance for the IVA, either on a 'full and final' basis (if you have the funds available, e.g. a pension lump-sum to cash in or third-party funding) or for regular payments, according to what is possible in the light of your resources.

The IVA normally lasts for five years, except in the case of a 'full and final', in which case you get a reasonable time from the date of the deal being finalised – up to 12 months – to come up with the funds.

Some insolvency practitioners make claims such as: "95% of your debts forgiven", i.e. the creditors would receive a dividend of only 5%, but such claims are often greatly exaggerated. Your IP will advise you what might be possible in your circumstances.

For setting up and administering an IVA, fees are chargeable by the IP out of the funds you will agree to make available to creditors. Generally you will not be required to fund any costs in advance of your arrangement being accepted.

Debt Management Plans (DMPs)

So-called Debt Management Plans (DMPs) fall within this chapter to some extent, depending on who sets them up and who is responsible for managing them.

If you decide to set up your own DMP, negotiate it yourself, and take responsibility for making the payments yourself, then that comes into what I call Plan C.

DMPs can be set up on your behalf by commercial companies, and there are many of them. The main benefits are that (a) they can negotiate a reduction of the debt and (b) once the plan is set up, you make a single monthly payment to the company, thus your money management is much simplified.

You don't have to deal with your creditors. The companies do of course charge for their services; typically 15% of the monthly payment, plus an administration fee to set up the plan, which could be equivalent of the first month's payment. This kind of informal arrangement is not legally binding, so it is more of a plan C solution.

With a commercially managed DMP there is no guarantee that the creditors will accept reduced payments or freeze interest, although that's the intention.

A DMP can, on the other hand, be set up on your behalf by one of the non-profit debt advice organisations; and lenders are more likely to accept one set up in this way rather than by you yourself. In some cases, e.g. with Consumer Credit Counselling Service, they will also manage the plan and make the payments on your behalf; in other cases you yourself take responsibility once the plan has been set up. However, if you yourself are taking responsibility for the payments, then I still call it Plan C, because you are still in touch with your creditors, even if you are benefiting from expert support.

There is also a kind of half-way house; National Debtline can advise you on a DMP and then pass the case on to a separate debt management company, which administers the plan and makes payments to your creditors. That company operates on a commercial footing but, unlike other such companies, will not charge you fees.

Pros and cons of externally supervised arrangements

Both bankruptcy and IVAs are legally binding. They both have the obvious advantage that parts of your debts are written off and you can start again. Another major advantage for many people is that, once you have agreed to one of these 'Plan B' options, the decisions are taken out of your hands and your creditors (with a few exceptions) cannot chase you for debts. That removes a lot of the stress that debtors feel.

In the past, bankruptcy was seen very much as a last resort when in debt. In recent years both the stigma and the practical disadvantages have lessened considerably.

If you are seriously considering bankruptcy but believe it still has a stigma, then an IVA may well appeal. However, like bankruptcy, IVAs are legally binding and your financial affairs will be closely scrutinised for a period, just as in bankruptcy. You are less likely to lose your home with an IVA but you might have to revalue it and give up part of the equity.

You might alternatively opt for a debt management plan, supervised by a debt management company; these are widely advertised. This might well be less onerous than bankruptcy or IVA in its restrictions upon you; however, it is not legally binding upon your creditors, so there is a danger that one or more of them might change their mind and chase you for a larger amount than was agreed. That cannot happen if you have filed for bankruptcy or if you have taken out an IVA, provided you have complied with the terms.

In general, the lower your assets and the lower your income, the less you have to lose by opting for bankruptcy or an IVA. But, at the risk of repetition, do not enter into either of these options without taking impartial advice. Your first port of call, if you prefer a face-to-face discussion with an adviser, might well be the Citizens Advice Bureau or an Insolvency Practitioner. Insolvency Practitioners will generally give you an initial free consultation outlining all options available to you and identifying the respective advantages, disadvantages and implications. Do remember that the ultimate choice of option must always be your own.

See the 'Resources' section of this book for a list of contact details of organisations that can help you. See also National Debtline's website for a useful table entitled 'Options for paying back your debts.'

What to do while you are considering Plan B

If you are 'insolvent within the meaning of the Insolvency Act 1986' or any later instrument, which means that 'your liabilities exceed your assets and that you are unable to pay your debts as they fall due', then you must consider your position very carefully and must avoid taking any actions that would be construed as offences if you were to be made bankrupt. These would include disposing of assets, reckless expenditure (hopefully you didn't need to be reminded of that at this stage!) or preferring one creditor over others.

In view of the 'not preferring one creditor…' aspect, it would probably be worthwhile informing your creditors that this is your situation, and asking them to freeze further interest and other charges while you discuss with your advisers and formulate a debt management plan.

I consulted several insolvency practitioners while I was deciding whether to go for Plan B; as I mentioned, many or most IPs offer a first consultation free of charge. The most professional of them recommended bankruptcy to me as "an option worth considering", though that practitioner's firm would have been able to bill me for more substantial fees if I had gone for an IVA instead. The cost to me personally of going bankrupt at that time would have been about £300 ($450); today it is £600 ($900). (There are, of course, trustee fees in the case of bankruptcy too but they are taken off the top of the share-out of assets).

Even though I personally didn't do it, there have been two major changes to the laws of England and Wales in the past ten years that make bankruptcy a more attractive option for many people. Those changes are the shorter period to discharge (12 months or less) and the changes that have made personal and occupational pension funds less 'available' to creditors.

It has occurred to me that those changes in pension legislation (in 2000) have a further effect: when one offers an IVA to creditors, or negotiates one's own deal, it is not unusual to point out to a creditor that if the plan cannot be agreed, then the debtor's only recourse would be to file for voluntary bankruptcy, in which case much less, or maybe nothing, would be forthcoming. With current legislation, such a statement is truer than ever.

Case studies

Tom Bowen

Tom, a self-employed contractor: filed for bankruptcy at county court, owing £70,000 ($105,000) with no assets. He had first been issued with a credit card at 18 and had run up these debts in 5 years. He will be discharged after a year. However, the easy credit that allowed Tom to get so deeply in debt is not generally available nowadays.

Mr & Mrs Bradshaw

A couple in their late 60s, whose combined pension income was £2,000 ($3,000) per month, had run up unsecured debts totalling £500,000 ($750,000) over 46 credit cards. The minimum payments alone for their cards totalled £12,000 ($18,000) per month. What is most remarkable is that their credit record remained impeccable but this surprising fact is not typical.

Colin Sexton

Colin Sexton is a salesman who got into financial difficulties when he lost two jobs in quick succession. Both had carried generous car allowances and, following the redundancies, he was forced to sell the vehicles quickly and at a loss. Debts were already mounting but the situation was compounded by poor financial decision-making, including taking out a high-interest consolidation loan.

Before long, he had a wallet full of credit cards and the situation had spiralled out of control. "I got myself stitched up a bit over the loan, but I can't blame anyone else but myself," says Mr Sexton. "A big element of the problem was the fact that I couldn't stop spending. Things went from bad to worse – when you've got behind on payments it's very hard to catch up." A keen golfer, Mr Sexton splashed out on top-of-the-range clubs and an expensive holiday to America with his wife. But he says it was the little things – clothes, going out for meals – that mounted up. "It all seemed very easy," he says. "Hardly a day would go by when I didn't receive a letter offering me more credit." Things came to a head when he had 9 credit cards and owed £60,000 ($90,000). "The people I had the loan with called one Saturday morning when I was out for a walk, and the reality of the situation suddenly hit me and stopped me in my tracks. I just thought, this is ridiculous, I can't carry on like this."

Mr S decided to take out an IVA, paying back 45p of every pound he owed over five years. "I'm over the moon that I decided to do this", he said. "It's not been easy and some of the creditors have been very aggressive. It will be very difficult to get credit again – but that's a good thing."

Michael Phillips

A city professional and the owner of an art gallery, Michael Phillips hardly ever missed a credit card payment and always met his mortgage commitments. But failure to keep up with the rent on the gallery business, into which Mr Phillips and his wife had invested their life savings, resulted in bankruptcy and the loss of the family home. "It was very difficult," said Mr Phillips. "We suddenly found ourselves transformed from a position where I was working in the city with no personal cash-flow issues to a situation when cash-flow became a massive issue."

A decision to give a personal guarantee on the five-year lease on the gallery meant that Mr P's landlord was able to present the family with a statutory demand. At the time, the Phillipses had missed 3 months' worth of payments. By the time they arrived in court, six months' later, the sum had risen to £25,000 ($37,500). The couple and their 12 year old daughter were instructed to leave their home and moved into temporary accommodation. Mr P said, "Everything went down to zero very, very fast. It came as quite a shock to the system. Bankruptcy is very hard. Although I have now been discharged, it does diminish your prospects of employment, especially the ones I am familiar with."

Mr Jackson

Mr Jackson had personal loans and credit cards totalling £37,000 ($55,500). He was living in rented accommodation with his wife and three children. Final demands were piling up; he had no assets. He approached a local debt advice centre for help and eventually decided to file for bankruptcy. While bankrupt he will not be able to obtain credit over £500 ($750) without disclosing the fact of his bankruptcy. He'll be discharged after a maximum period of 12 months, but the bankruptcy order would be registered with credit reference agencies for at least six years. Even after that time he might still be asked if he's ever been bankrupt before when applying for some credit, particularly a mortgage. He might also have difficulty gaining a new tenancy agreement through an agency if the family have to move.

Despite the restrictions, Mr Jackson felt this was the best route out of debt. After paying £450 ($675) to petition successfully for his own bankruptcy he said "A big cloud has been lifted. It's the best thing I have ever done." The fact that Mr Jackson had no assets will have been a significant factor in the debt centre's advice.

How to find an Insolvency Practitioner

If you feel that Plan B could well fit your situation, then you will need to consult an insolvency practitioner (IP). Here is a checklist to help you locate the right IP: it has been provided by, and is reproduced by permission of, insolvency practitioner Melanie Giles of PJG Recovery, Cardiff.

When you have recognised that you are suffering financial difficulties and feel there is nowhere to turn, there is now a wealth of firms offering advice as either insolvency practitioners, debt management companies or charitable operations. Many of these companies operate with extensive marketing budgets, and the media is full of companies offering to assist you to write off substantial portions of your debts. To the untrained eye, the decision as to which company to instruct can be daunting, in an area where there is yet such a degree of conflicting advice. If you feel that you are unable to cope with the financial pressure any more, it is usually wise to obtain two or three options in order to find a balanced view. But what sort of things should you ask an advisor in order to arrive at a decision to instruct them? I have listed a few pointers which should help.

1 What solutions do you offer? Most firms specialise in either Individual Voluntary Arrangements (IVA) or Debt Management Plans (DMP). As such, the advice you receive may well be biased towards the core business of that particular firm, and you may not receive adequate advice as to the advantages of all options available to you. Make sure the advisor you choose counsels you on the implications, advantages and disadvantages of bankruptcy, IVA's and DMP. Beware anyone who tells you what you should do straight away – but favour those who recommend that you have a good think about all options and choose the right solution. Bear in mind that the wider the options available at each advice firm, the more likely you are to get best advice and choose the right solution.

2 What procedure should I choose? From your chats with the advisors, does it feel to you that clear ethical procedures are in place and followed by all staff who will be working on your case? Is the firm able to provide you with feedback from other clients; have they received positive or negative feedback on the iva.co.uk forum, and have they given you the opportunity of a face to face meeting? Do you generally get a gut feeling that the firm is going to act in your best interests, or are they only interested in taking

your money? Ask your creditors if they have heard of the advisor, and do they have any positive or negative comments to make. Ask them what their track record success rate is at creditor meeting approvals and successfully completed proposals. Importantly, you must ensure that the firm of your choice is fully compliant with current protocols.

3   At what point will you recommend a solution? Are they telling you to do an IVA before they have gathered up all of the information from you and conducted a detailed telephone or face to face interview? You should be wary if they have not fully investigated your personal circumstances prior to providing advice. Anyone who comes up with a sensible solution in less than half an hour is probably being motivated by selling you a specific product rather than finding the right solution to suit your circumstances.

4   Do you charge for advice? You should be wary about paying for advice until you have agreed upon a solution. Many advisors would prefer to see you paying contributions straight away, even when your proposals are being researched and prepared. This is a good way of ascertaining whether you can afford the payments prior to committing formally to a repayment plan; however, do ensure that your advisor offers you a full money back guarantee in the event that the solution is not acceptable to your creditors, or you change your mind. After all, this money is money which should be held in trust for your creditors at the end of the day.

5   What is the process? How much work is the advisor actually going to be doing for you? Will you be left to fill in complicated and lengthy documents on your own? Will they write to your creditors and

deal with queries in the meantime? Can you ring them at any time for advice? What is the timescale for completing the work? Are they going to refer you on to another advisor?

6   Only choose a firm appropriately licensed by the Financial Conduct Authority.

Before you contact the company have a detailed list of your creditors and a household budget showing your income and expenditure (not including unsecured debt repayments) to hand. Also make up a checklist of questions you wish to ask, and then you can compare the answers in making your final judgement. Remember you have to work with these guys perhaps for the next five years, so the 'marriage' must feel right and you must be assured that they are going to look after your interests as well as those of the creditors in the long term.

"Budget: a mathematical confirmation of your suspicions." – A A Latimer

Finally...

Advantages of "Plan B" solutions:
* Removal of stress: your creditors can't pursue you.
* Legally binding.
* Fresh start.

Disadvantages:
* Loss of credit rating.
* Perceived stigma?
* Possible loss of home.
* Official scrutiny of your affairs.

**"Money will buy you a pretty good dog, but it won't buy the wag of his tail."
– Henry Wheeler Shaw**

Plan C
Negotiate a Deal

10

Settle a proportion of the debts in return for the balance being written off…but negotiate the deal yourself.

If you don't believe you can achieve Plan A and you don't want the external control of Plan B, there is an alternative, which your coach/counsellor/adviser can develop with you. This alternative would enable you to offer your non-priority creditors a better and more acceptable deal than Plan B – certainly more acceptable to them than bankruptcy – but it will depend upon your being able to manage the whole thing yourself and deal with creditors direct. It's what I call Plan C. (I might have called it 'The Third Way' if I were a politician). It involves your making an offer to pay an agreed proportion of every debt, in return for the creditor writing off the balance.

National Debtline's website calls Plan C an 'informally negotiated arrangement with creditors' and that's a good description in one way, because it flags up a significant disadvantage of a Plan C solution, which is that the arrangements you make are not legally binding. The consequence of this is that your creditors might decide at a later stage that they could have got a better deal from you, and chase you for more. (It happened to me in one or two cases. After a little more correspondence, things were back on track. However, it can happen.) By comparison, if you enter into an IVA, for example, provided 75% of the creditors (by value) agree, the agreement is legally binding on all of them, even those who did not agree. I have not used the National Debtline 'informally negotiated' description, partly because the word 'informal' might give you the idea that this is an easy option. It is not; you will have to be totally professional in your dealings and will have to write lots of letters.

Of course the fact that a Plan C solution is not legally binding could in some circumstances help you. If, for example, you had agreed instalment payments which at the time were affordable, but then your income fell – not an impossible scenario in today's economic climate – it might be possible to go back and renegotiate the deal without one or more of your creditors forcing you into bankruptcy, given that that is what you had decided to avoid.

You must feel able to 'manage the whole thing yourself' because you will make all the decisions and you will remain in direct contact with your creditors, but you don't need to work alone and without support. There is plenty of knowledgeable support available to help you evaluate your situation, tell you what kinds of offers might be acceptable to your creditors and provide you with backup in a variety of ways. You'll find contact details in the Resources section.

What you'll be doing in effect is setting up, and then administering, your own Debt Management Plan. DMPs that are supervised by an officially appointed person were covered in the last chapter and a key feature of such plans is that all creditors have to receive the same offer, i.e. the same 'dividend' (pence in the pound, cents on the dollar, etc). I recommend that you do exactly the same when you are handling the whole thing yourself: it might not be a legal requirement but it will definitely be a key element of your ability to sell the deal to your creditors. Even if there might be some that you want to offer a better deal, e.g. if you owed money to a friend, (as I did) or to a trade creditor, maybe a small local business that you wanted to treat more favourably than, say, a major credit-card provider or bank, you cannot offer one group of creditors 50 pence in the pound, for example, and another group 25 pence. That might seem desirable to you but could invalidate the deal. So be sure that you make it clear you are offering the same deal to everyone. Human nature being what it is, no creditor will want to feel that someone else is getting a better deal, irrespective of the legalities of the thing.

Priority debts

While you were doing your reality check you will, I hope, have classified your debts into priority and non-priority. Priority debts will mostly, if not totally, consist of any arrears you may have built up in the essential areas of keeping a roof over your head (mortgage or rent), the associated taxes (Council Tax in Great Britain or domestic rates in Northern Ireland) and essential utilities, i.e. gas, electricity and water. (Phone rental has often been classed as a utility but it doesn't qualify as a priority debt for this purpose, whether it is landline or mobile or broadband). There are also some other categories of arrears that could in the worst case land you in prison for non-payment, so we class them as priority debts too; they include court fines and child maintenance.

Everything I say, therefore, about 'negotiating a deal' for partial forgiveness of debts in return for a pro-rata offer to pay a certain amount, applies to non-priority debts. The priority debts you will have to pay in full, unless there are unusual extenuating circumstances; non-payment could lead to your losing your home or, in the worst case, your freedom. And, as I have mentioned elsewhere, income tax arrears also count as a priority debt and would count as a first charge on your estate if you were to become bankrupt.

Although you will in general have to pay all priority debts in full, there will be a need to negotiate for time. Therefore what I say in this chapter about negotiating does indeed apply to all types of debts.

If you have mortgage or rent arrears, refer back to the relevant sections in Chapter 8. Those debts deserve the same priority whether you are going for Plan A or Plan C.

Negotiating non-priority debts

If you decide to go down the Plan C route then of course there are negotiations involved. Plan A involved negotiating for time to pay but this one is more complicated in that it means negotiating not only for time while you put the deal together, but also for a discounted settlement on the non-priority debts. Your creditors, however, may be prepared to freeze further interest payments and late-payment charges, while you are putting your plan together and also while you are in the process of paying off any deal that might be agreed.

It may be that you have some funds available and could make an offer for 'full and final settlement'. The word 'full' in this context means that the debt is acknowledged by the creditor as being 'paid in full' or 'satisfied in full'; you are paying a lump sum, though you are paying less than the full amount. The funds you have available might come from friends and family, or maybe from the lump-sum element of cashing in an occupational pension, depending on your age (I was lucky enough – and old enough – to be able to do the latter). More usually, though, you'll make an offer for payment in instalments.

However, if you do decide to go for 'full and final settlement,' then bear in mind that you will be negotiating on several fronts and not everyone will agree at the same time; a tricky situation. What you want to avoid at all costs is to have agreed with some creditors, paid them the lump sums agreed, and then to be forced into bankruptcy anyway if other substantial creditors would not agree to a negotiated settlement. That's why you'll find that one of my standard letters in 'Resources' caters for the situation where you have agreed a deal with one or more creditors but need to delay payment of the sum agreed pending agreement from other creditors. For this particular strategy, therefore – i.e. Plan C offering lump-sum for full and final settlement – my usual warning is louder than ever: take advice.

Some creditors will be reasonable and flexible but others will be intransigent and will play hardball. However, once you have decided that you are going to take action about your debt situation, you should inform your creditors of your situation and ask them for a moratorium on interest and charges.

At the risk of yet more repetition, this is where I say again, "don't negotiate on the phone; do it in writing." It is simply not necessary to pick up the phone whenever creditors phone with demands and threats; that is a stress you can do without. In Chapter 2 ('Mind over matter') I discussed the extra stress of dealing with phone demands; even if you might say that you can handle the stress, there is another very practical reason for doing it this way. If you negotiate on the phone, and if at a later date you find that the creditor's recall of that conversation is not the same as yours (surprise, surprise), you will have no record of what was said or what was agreed. So let those calls go through to voicemail, but then respond promptly in writing to any messages left. Do it all in writing; it's more work, of course, but the outcomes – not only for your debt management plan but also for your state of mind – will be better.

Needless to say, keep copies of everything. The fact that you are able to refer to the content and the dates of all previous correspondence is worth its weight in gold. Get that lever-arch file; if you have many creditors you'll soon fill it. Of course you will have kept copies of your outgoing letters on your computer, but when you go for meetings with your adviser it will be very helpful for that adviser to be able to scan a paper record of all the correspondence, both incoming and outgoing.

Something I learned is that, while you are negotiating with a creditor, they might simultaneously instruct intermediaries to collect on their behalf. This might be policy, it might not, so be aware of the fact that the left hand might not know what the right is doing within the creditor company. If this happens, simply refer them back to previous correspondence (even sending copies of it) in a polite way. This way you retain, if not the moral high ground, at least the efficient high ground. Don't assume everyone is super-efficient. Poor communication within a creditor company and between them and their intermediaries can work in your favour, if you are patient.

Another word of warning. Even when a creditor has confirmed in writing that the debt is 'satisfied', that is not always the end of that particular branch of the road, although it should be. One of my debts was confirmed in writing as satisfied but then that same creditor started to chase me for the balance three years later.

I assumed that this was a case of the left hand not knowing what the right was doing, i.e. it was an error rather than bad faith, thus I implied as much in my letter. Eventually the matter was concluded satisfactorily. There were two lessons here: (a) persistence pays, and (b) the size of a company is no guarantee of its efficiency and the quality of its internal communications, so be aware these things can happen.

Now for 'the $64,000 question', as we used to say: how much are you going to offer to your creditors? Only you and your adviser(s) can answer that question, but first you have to do the 'Reality' exercise described in Chapter 5. Your adviser can tell you what 'dividend' might be acceptable in the market conditions that apply when you're reading this book…but only when you have calculated your discretionary income will you know how much you could afford to offer.

Third-party involvement – 'Negotiating with limited authority'
Back in the 1950s, the Americans and the Soviets were negotiating arms reduction treaties. The very different negotiating styles of the two sides have provided rich pickings for students of the art and science of negotiating. Put simply, the more upfront Americans liked to see themselves, or at least present themselves, as the decision-makers as well as the negotiators. The Russians' style was quite different; more devious or more patient or more subtle, depending on your viewpoint. Even if their negotiator knew exactly what the 'bottom line' was, his response to any new proposal would be, "let me take this proposal back to the Kremlin and see if they can accept it".

So – who is your equivalent of the Kremlin? Hopefully you have a third party helping you in this process. If you don't have access to an adviser right now, create an imaginary one: the famous 'straw man.' So, for any new proposal from a creditor, you can be like that Russian negotiator – "Thank you for this proposal (or counter-proposal). I have to discuss it with my adviser". That buys you time, while not sacrificing the high ground.

I have said that if your debt problem is serious, I believe it is important to be someone who always responds Promptly, Politely and Professionally. Then you should also be Persistent. In other words, stick to your guns; employing the 'broken record' technique when necessary, unless you (or your adviser) finally decide, after a number of exchanges, that the proposal you have made will definitely not succeed.

That broken record technique includes never being afraid to repeat what you've said in a previous letter, if their response appears to ignore something you've said. Many people (and companies) don't really read or take notice of things the first time. So if you don't get the response you want, just repeat yourself in the next letter, and so on.

Seeing both sides

The result of this process should ideally be a negotiated agreement with your creditors that is acceptable to all parties.

But what if you are unable to negotiate such an agreement? Back in the 90s, I used to run courses in negotiation and other business communication skills. At that time, one of the questions discussed between professional negotiators and their clients was: "What's our best alternative to a negotiated agreement?"

In other words, what's our fall-back position?

To recap: the main options in dealing with debt can be summarised as follows:

- **Plan A** ('Pay It All') – Reduce your expenditure and/or increase your income so as to pay off 100% of your debts over a period that's acceptable to your creditors.
- **Plan B** ('Out Of Your Hands') – File for voluntary bankruptcy or enter into an IVA (Individual Voluntary Arrangement), or its equivalent where you live, or any other kind of legally binding and externally supervised debt management plan.
- **Plan C** ('Negotiate a deal') – (i.e. this chapter). Negotiate with your non-priority creditors yourself (with or without

the help of a debt adviser), to write off part of the debt and pay the rest either as a lump-sum or in instalments. However such deals are not legally binding.

But what about your creditors' options? It is worth giving this some thought. I'll go further and say that you could usefully write down what you think their options are in your particular situation. The act of writing it down will probably reduce your stress level. Some examples:

- They may seek a court judgment against you.
- They may seek to force you into *in*voluntary bankruptcy.
- Priority creditors might seek to repossess property if the debt is secured against it.

Before you get too worried about the last item on that list, bear in mind that repossession will be viewed as a very last resort by any reputable company, assuming your main creditors are either financial services providers (banks, credit card companies etc) or trade creditors. In these days of 24-hour news and online discussion boards, companies are very careful about their public image. There would also be considerable legal costs for them, so there might not be enough value in the asset to make it worthwhile to repossess. However, if you think that this is even a remote possibility, then take professional advice immediately.

The above options may satisfy the creditor's pride, but will those options realise any more money for them than the negotiated agreement you propose? Let's hope that you can convince them that the negotiated deal is best. If you become bankrupt as a result of your proposals failing, then the outcome for your creditors will in all likelihood be considerably worse. It is worth remembering that, and even reminding any particularly intransigent creditors of the fact that the negotiated agreement is better for all concerned than your becoming bankrupt.

If a debt is secured on your property, then of course the creditor has that extra option of repossessing that property, even if they are reluctant to exercise it. Thus you should be careful about offers for a 'debt-consolidation loan', no matter how attractive the terms in the short term, if it has to be secured against your home.

If a creditor sends you a 'notice of court action', it is not necessarily a cause for panic. These kinds of letters are often just a way of scaring you into settling this particular debt before all the others you might have. The threat is rarely carried out. Such letters are often sent with a second-class stamp; if you see that, it would be clear evidence, or at least a clue, that the threat is not serious. The only document to worry about would be an actual court summons: happily, these are few and far between. If you get one of those, and preferably well before that point, then take advice without delay.

A final and most important point: the agreement that you propose to creditors has to be acceptable to your partner/family as well as to you. So I urge you to be honest with your partner. Many people try to hide debt problems from their 'nearest and dearest', often with tragic results.

If you decide you want to try 'Plan C'; as I did, here's a key question before deciding on that option: "Do you feel able to deal with this yourself – even with the support of an adviser – especially as the process of negotiation might well take many months and you might well be under considerable pressure while doing it?" If the answer is yes, then how will you motivate yourself and maintain that motivation? Here are some ideas:

- Make a list of the benefits that will accrue from your new debt-free state when you've achieved it; the longer the list, the more energy and motivation you will have to continue with your plan.
- Don't forget the support of friends can be crucial, but they can only help if you let them.
- There are also benefits that will accrue even sooner, i.e. during the *process* of dealing with your debts. 'The best things in life are free' but too often we forget that old

saying. Many of the joys of life don't cost anything, e.g. reading, (why not visit your local library?) walking and sex. Personally, I rediscovered the fun of cooking while cutting down the costs of eating out. I gave up my car and I found I met lots more people, because I wasn't cocooned in a car all the time. You might find lots of fun ways to spend time with your partner, and /or your children, that don't cost money. See also Chapter 11.

- Think of an image that represents the new debt-free, financially solvent you; find a picture of that and put it on your wall or download it onto your PC as your screen-saver. A word of caution: if the first image you think of is a fantastic new car, for which you'd have to take out a large new loan, then find a different image!

- Finally: acknowledge that this process will become stressful at times. When that happens, remind yourself of the good things in your life. Money is not everything.

If your answer is yes, you can handle this, then remember that you are dealing with people, even though the letters may seem to come from a faceless and heartless bureaucracy and even though I've advised you to avoid speaking to these people except by letter or possibly e-mail. Someone, somewhere, is going to decide whether to accept your offer, and that person's decision will depend to some extent on how he or she perceives you, and their judgment as to whether his or her employer can do better than the offer you are making. This is a classic example of positive expectations producing positive results. If you make your proposal in a way that suggests that you think it might be refused, then it probably will be. As Henry Ford famously said: "If you think you can…or you think you can't…you're probably right".

If you feel that you couldn't handle all this yourself, but Plan C is definitely the way you want to go, then turn to the Resources section and get help from one of the organisations listed there.

The taxman

The dreaded taxman (HMRC in the UK, the IRS in the States, etc) has a primary claim on your estate, i.e. your assets. In most circumstances you can negotiate only for time with this most persistent of creditors.

Even if it does nothing else, copious correspondence buys you time while you, and your accountant or financial adviser if you have one, find ways to reduce the liability. For example, if you are self-employed, you may have had losses in previous years that can be brought forward.

So if that could be your situation, consult an accountant. Don't say you can't afford to; I believe you can't afford not to, unless the amount of your debt to the taxman is trivial.

"Intaxication: Euphoria at getting a tax refund, which lasts until you realise it was your money to start with." – From a *Washington Post* word contest

Case studies

Miss Peters

Miss P had an unsecured loan and overdraft with a well-known high street bank. She got into financial difficulty when she came out of employment and became dependent on benefits. She experienced severe mental health problems which incapacitated her to the degree of being unable to manage money effectively. The nature of her condition was confirmed by her medical practitioner.

The bureau looked into the circumstances surrounding the borrowing. At the time the loan was taken out there was considerable doubt as to her capacity to make an informed decision of this kind. Although the bank had encouraged the borrowing, for which there appeared no obvious purpose to justify the burden of repayment with interest; in all probability their representatives would not have reasonably been aware of her medical condition. Nevertheless the bureau were able to negotiate full `write off` totalling about £14,000 ($21,000) on the basis of medical evidence and the ongoing nature of the client's condition

(Author's note: this is an unusual case, in which 100% write-off was negotiated by Citizens Advice. The debtor therefore did not have to take responsibility for making any payments, which a debtor normally has to do with a Plan C-type solution. A totally satisfactory outcome for the debtor and the moral is, as I have said many times elsewhere, take advice!)

Mike Allen & Barbara Spiller

A couple with two children who started off with a £3,500 ($5,250) bank loan to pay for a new car. He lost his job, so his partner went to the bank to explain that they could not keep up the payments. She was told by the bank that she should take out another loan on which she herself could make the repayments. The couple ended up taking out five loans in the manner and debt built up to £30,000 ($45,000). Citizens Advice says that the couple did not get cash to spend; all the money went on paying the debts.

Citizens Advice took the case to the Ombudsman; £20,000 ($30,000) of the debt was written off and the remaining £10,000 ($15,000) is being paid back at the rate of £1/month. The moral: consult Citizens Advice.

James Ellison

James Ellison's business collapsed after he'd put £200,000 ($300,000) into the company. When he dissolved the company he had to apply for benefits. By that time he'd remortgaged but unfortunately he found that housing benefit only paid the original mortgage. Hence he quickly went into arrears on the mortgage and the lender applied to repossess. The local debt advice office helped with information, came to court and negotiated successfully for him. Despite being an accountant, Mr E says that without this help he would have lost his home.

Mrs Hanson

Mrs H, who, having to care for her grandchild (which she'd been asked to do by Social Services) and consequent loss of income, had accumulated rent arrears of £800 ($1,200), utility arrears and over £1,000 ($1,500) in Council Tax arrears too. Her income was only £95 ($143) per week, out of which she had to pay Council Tax of £23 ($35) per week (Aren't cases like this an argument for replacing the UK's Council Tax system with a local income tax? "You might well think that: I couldn't possibly comment.") and rent of £60 ($90) per week. The local advice centre was able to help Mrs H get benefits which she'd been entitled to claim but which she had previously been denied. This action doubled her income to £200 ($300) per week but the debts had to be cleared and there was much negotiation before that was achieved. An unexpected bonus from the advice centre's intervention was that Social Services agreed to train social workers on the need to inform clients of their rights. Moral: the negotiating power of the advice agencies is invaluable. 'Advice' is only a part of what they can do.

"If money is your hope for independence you will never have it. The only real security that a man will have in this world is a reserve of knowledge, experience, and ability." – Henry Ford

Finally...

- Tell your wife/husband/partner.
- *Don't* take phone calls from creditors. *Do* respond to phone messages, but do it in writing.
- Reply to all creditor demands in writing: Promptly, Politely, Professionally, setting out your situation and (if you know) what you propose to do or what you need from them (e.g. more info, more time, interest freeze, etc), and above all be Persistent; you might not get what you want the first time.

- My recommendation to reply to letters promptly applies even if you can't meet the demand.
- Keep copies of all correspondence.
- Ignore threats (rarely carried out) but always reply 'promptly, politely and professionally'.
- Do deal with the priority debts first; these will be arrears on rent or mortgage, utility bills (gas & electricity), Council Tax, court fines, child maintenance etc, and you will generally have to pay these in full. Your Plan C negotiations will, in general, only apply to non-priority debts.
- Make a 'token offer' of some sort: even £1/month shows willing while you put together a proposal.
- There's free advice available, so use it. An adviser's support and procedures will add legitimacy to your case; also you are then 'negotiating with limited authority'. Refer everything to your adviser.
- If you don't have an adviser, negotiate as if you did.
- When negotiating with creditors, the 'broken record' technique is often effective. Repetition, repetition, repetition…(you get the point).
- When you make an offer to non-priority creditors, it must be 'pro rata', i.e. you should make the same offer to all (expressed as a percentage or pence in the pound). State that your offer is conditional upon your getting the agreement of a majority of creditors.
- Health warning: deals you have negotiated yourself are not legally binding. That cuts both ways but most debtors will see it as a risk rather than an opportunity. If you are risk-averse you might therefore decide not to go for Plan C.

"A rich man is nothing but a poor man with money." – WC Fields

Decision Time 11

The way forward

What's the best option for you? When will you start to implement it? What's your plan of action?

The final stage of the coach's eye picture of dealing with debt – or of solving any problem, in fact – is this: you have decided on your goal(s) and reviewed your current reality; you have identified all your options to bridge the gap between them; you have obtained and evaluated any extra information you needed but didn't have at the start; now it is decision time. Now you have to decide which option you will choose, make a plan of action, and motivate yourself to take the actions necessary.

By now it might be obvious to you which option or options will suit your situation. I believe the best solution for most debt situations lies within one of the three groups that I described as follows:

- **Plan A** – Find ways to pay all your debts in full, within a timeframe acceptable to your creditors.
- **Plan B** – File for bankruptcy; or enter into an IVA or equivalent legally-binding arrangement; meanwhile handling over supervision of your affairs to a third party for a period of between one and five years.
- **Plan C** – Negotiate with your non-priority creditors to pay those debts partially, within an agreed timeframe, in return for the balance being written off.

Whichever you choose, it almost goes without saying that while you are implementing your plan you will need to maximise your discretionary income, i.e. increase your income and/or reduce your spending, and be seen by your creditors to be doing so.

The power of questions again

In this book I've said many times I believe in the power of questions. I love those lines from a poem of Rudyard Kipling, who clearly believed in it too:

I keep six honest serving-men
(They taught me all I knew);
Their names are What and Why and When
And How and Where and Who.

Like Kipling, I have always believed in the power of so-called 'open questions' – you know, the ones that you can't answer with a 'yes' or a 'no', or even a 'maybe'. It is our answers to open questions that help us to summon up the courage to get started ("screw our courage to the sticking-point", to quote the Bard).

As an alternative to Kipling, I offer this story from a Nobel-prize-winning physicist (or maybe mathematician: I can't remember which). He was being interviewed on the BBC a few years ago and the interviewer was looking for facts about his childhood environment which might have contributed to his success. His answer was wonderful: "When I got home from school every day, my mother would greet me with: 'Did you ask any good questions today?'"

The 'good questions' for you at this point might well include the following:

- Which option will work for you?
- What's your plan?
- Do you have the belief and will-power to do what is required? If not, how will you motivate yourself?
- Who can help you?

And, last but definitely not least:

- What's the first step and when will you take it?

Decision criteria

One of the most basic principles of coaching is that the client (that's you) has the answers and resources he or she needs. All the coach needs to do (that's me, for the purposes of this virtual conversation we're having) is to ask the right questions. If you had your own personal coach or debt counsellor, their job would be to help to give you focus and remind you of your answers to 'all those questions', every time you lose your way. And repeat the questions if necessary.

Most coaches say that only the client can make the decisions but of course the coach can listen, help clarify the thinking process (by asking all those questions) and help also by providing information that might be missing. However, when you are trying to decide between the different types of solutions, there are certain criteria that *could* (not should, only could) sway you in one direction or another.

Do you own your home?

If you do, and especially if you have a substantial chunk of equity in the property, then your home will be vulnerable in a bankruptcy; see Chapter 9. Therefore Plan B will be less attractive to you.

What's the total value of your assets?

As above, the higher the value of your assets the less attractive Plan B will be to you. Conversely, the lower the value of your assets at the time you are faced with this decision, the more feasible Plan B might be; however, at this point you absolutely need to take advice.

In this situation plan C would also come into the reckoning, because if you are someone who could well consider making themselves voluntarily bankrupt, then your creditors will bear this in mind and thus would probably give more favourable consideration to any offer you might make. That's because in a bankruptcy they would probably recover very little.

Do you have a substantial private/occupational pension pot?

Pensions used to be more vulnerable in bankruptcy a decade ago than they are now, especially if they did not have so-called 'protected rights'. Things are better nowadays from the viewpoint of the debtor; even so, take specialist advice.

Do you have dependent children?

If so, and if you own your own home, then this would probably incline you away from Plan B.

The effect of debt problems on any dependent children is an important issue, not just because of the threat of repossession. Some of the economies that you want to make may cause disputes because of the peer pressure that children live under these days. I do not underestimate these issues but probably the best strategy is to take the whole family into your confidence about the situation, no matter how hard that may be to do. That assumes that the children are old enough to understand, of course. As you probably know if you are a parent, children are very adaptable. If you give them an opportunity to share in the responsibility of achieving what you want to achieve, you may be surprised at what they'll do to help.

What's the size of your debts relative to your income?

…especially relative to discretionary income. The smaller this ratio, the more likely is Plan A to be attractive and achievable. The larger it is, the more attractive will be Plans B or C.

The term 'consumer leverage ratio' is sometimes used by lenders to describe the ratio of total household debt to *disposable* income, i.e. income net of tax. I have stressed the importance of knowing your *discretionary* income, i.e. net income after essential living costs; however, disposable income (income after tax) is also an important measure because everything below that line is, in a lender's eyes, subject to decisions by you, the borrower. 'Essential' living costs are, after all, subject to value judgements about what is and is not essential. And a creditor's judgements might not coincide with yours.

Are you currently unemployed? If so, do you envisage it being long-term?

This would, other things being equal, make Plan B – and specifically bankruptcy – more feasible; or, at least, less damaging to you.

Last question, but definitely not least: what kind of person are you?

By this I mean your attitude to risk. If you are what a financial adviser, if he or she were suggesting investments to you, would call 'risk-averse', then Plan C will be less attractive because it is not legally binding. I have dealt with this in more detail in Chapter 10.

Belief and will-power

In an earlier chapter I said that goals should be achievable. When you've considered your options and decided on your plan of action, how sure are you that you actually will perform the actions necessary to reach the goal? If you are not absolutely sure or very sure, then maybe the goal is wrong for you, or the timeframe is unrealistic. In that situation, you probably will not do what's necessary, and then you'll demotivate yourself by concluding you are unable to break the cycle of debt. In such a case, reframe your goal to something less ambitious, or spread the actions out over a longer timeframe, or break the goal down into more manageable chunks. "Anyone can eat an elephant; one bite at a time."

Turning your decision into a plan

In an earlier chapter I talked about the idea of writing the question, "how can I get from where I am now to where I want to be?" and then forcing yourself to write lots of answers. You could use the same technique here; having decided what option, i.e. what strategy, you are going to follow, write yourself another question at the top of another sheet of paper. For example: "What needs to happen for me to get to my goal by means of…" (whatever option you have decided on)? Again, force yourself to write as many answers as you can. Then delete the ones that won't work, give the remaining ones deadlines, put them in chronological order, and then you have a plan.

For example, if you have decided that Plan A is the *strategy* you will follow, your *action steps* might be:

• Consult an independent non-profit debt adviser;
• Write to all your creditors advising your situation and asking for time to formulate a plan;
• Propose a payback timetable.

…and so on.

If, on the other hand, you wanted to consider 'Plan B: Out Of Your Hands', read chapter 9 again. Then your first action step would be to consult an adviser; you might well have a general discussion of all the options with one of the advice charities but then you'll need to consult an insolvency practitioner (IP). Then you'll draw up your action plan in consultation with that IP.

To find an IP in your area, search the official online database whose web address you'll find in 'Resources'. Then to select the right one for your needs, see the checklist at the end of Chapter 9.

On the other hand, you might prefer to try Plan C. If so, here's a key question before deciding on that option: "Do you feel able to deal with this yourself – even with the support of an adviser – especially as the process of negotiation might well take many months and you might well be under considerable pressure while doing it?" If the answer is yes, then how will you motivate yourself and maintain that motivation? Taking that independent advice will again be your first step.

One of the essential prerequisites to summoning up the

willpower to deal with debt in a significant way and to stay out of debt is to re-evaluate your attitudes to the 'needs versus wants' question. So many of the things that we think we need (and have been convinced by advertisers that we really do need) are in fact wants, not needs. If push came to shove, could you do without them? If getting out of debt is really important to you, then perhaps you could do without some of these wants, as I did. After a surprisingly short period I adjusted my attitude and I found I was perfectly happy without those former so-called needs.

Finally...

- Before making your decision, ensure that you have in front of you all relevant information.
- Set aside some quiet time to review your goal, your current reality and your options – with your adviser if you have one – make a decision and stick to it.
- If you own your own home it is more likely to be vulnerable in a Plan B type solution. Plan B is therefore even less attractive if you also have dependent children.

"A pessimist sees the difficulty in every opportunity. An optimist sees the opportunity in every difficulty." – Winston Churchill

Keep up the Good Work 12

How to prevent debt recurring

How will you ensure you don't fall right back into debt?

- Can you boost your income? Maybe.
- Can you cut your expenditure? Probably.

There is little point in eliminating your debts if, within a short time, you are back in the same situation, so this chapter suggests some ways to reduce expenditure. Of course, finding ways to increase income can achieve the same effect, but will probably take longer.

The benefits of concentrating your efforts on reducing expenditure are twofold. Firstly, it's a strategy from which you can start benefiting immediately, whereas finding new sources of income takes time. Secondly, a time-honoured lesson from business: "cost savings go straight to the bottom line".

In other words, your discretionary income is immediately improved by exactly the same amount you saved by spending less money. Extra income, on the other hand, does not all go straight to your personal 'bottom line' for two simple reasons: firstly, you will pay tax on the difference and secondly, you might incur extra costs to generate that income, even if it's something simple like extra travel costs.

My apologies if that last paragraph is obvious to you; it wasn't obvious to me for a long time, even though I ran my own business with some success for quite a few years.

Cutting your costs will, in many cases, lead to a greener lifestyle too, so there is a double benefit. You can be saving the planet while saving your bank-balance.

You might say: "I want to cut my expenditure but don't know where to start."

Before we start, here's a health warning. Most of the content of this chapter you probably know already. But knowing it and doing it are two different things. As the old farmer said to the salesman trying to sell him books on new developments in agriculture: "Young man, I already know how to farm twice as well as I do." So please treat this chapter as revision, not new learning.

Can budgeting be fun?

At first sight, that seems a stupid question. For most of us (including me in the past) the idea of creating and sticking to a budget was somewhere just short of tooth extraction without anaesthetic. But it's now my contention that it can be fun; provided you 'start with the end in mind'. In other words to have in mind what you might do in the future with the money you'll save by effective budgeting. In this way, budgeting could even be aspirational: a revolutionary idea if there ever was one.

First of all, I suggest you create an expenditure log; for two weeks make a note of everything you spend. That will tell you where your money is going and will perhaps give you some ideas of where savings could be made.

In this age of the smartphone, there are of course some very effective and simple-to-use apps to help you do that. See the Resources section.

The cash economy

Elsewhere in this book (see Chapter 8) I've said that you are more likely to keep an eye on your spending if you go back to the good old-fashioned (some might even say 'archaic') method of paying for stuff with cash. I think the message is important enough to be repeated.

Nowadays we are so used to using cards for most things, therefore I am no longer amazed, as I used to be, when I see people using a card for something costing a fiver. It's very convenient to pay with a card, of course; but it's a sure-fire way to overspend. I know, for example, that if I pay with plastic at the supermarket it doesn't feel the same as if I pay with cash. Moreover I am more likely to avoid 'impulse buys' if I have decided in advance to pay with cash.

If we buy with plastic, it doesn't feel as if we are really spending. So how about 'getting back to the cash economy'?

Try this:

Make sure you have Direct Debits only for all regular *and essential* expenditure. Then use the table in the Resources section to do a budget. Decide from that information how much cash you are going to allow yourself. Draw that amount in cash on the same day every week, and don't draw more; and leave your cards at home (unless you are travelling and need one for emergencies) and don't go over your cash limit. Then your spending will seem more real.

To begin with, it'll be hard. You'll often reach the end of the money before the end of the week. But when you've got into the habit of thrift, you might be pleasantly surprised to find it fun; especially if you keep constantly in mind what you're going to achieve and what benefits that will bring you.

I suggested leaving all your cards at home when you are out and about. If you want to be really ruthless, cut them up (but keep the accounts open in case of future need)…except for your **debit** card for minor emergencies; and **one** credit card (the one with the lowest interest rate) for major emergencies or planned major expenditures (e.g. holidays) when you know you can repay the balance in full by the next statement date.

But try to leave even those two at home on days when your schedule is predictable, e.g. from home to work and back home again. That way you are removing yourself from temptation and you become more aware of your spending patterns.

I mention budgeting apps in the Resources section of this book. They will also help you to become more aware of your patterns.

Mortgage

When did you last review it? Of course you might have a 'tie-in', due to a superb deal you negotiated six months ago. If not, talk to a broker or financial adviser, or look online or at your weekend newspaper's money pages for info on the best deals on mortgages, insurance and any other financial products. You already knew this, I am sure.

Rent

If you are a private tenant, the next time your landlord asks you for a rent increase, say you can't afford it. It would cost him money and hassle to replace you, so he might reconsider. Many landlords simply increase the rent at each review point as a knee-jerk reaction, assuming that, like everything else, rents should always increase. Do your research before the review day; even if you don't want to move under any circumstances, being prepared could get you a better deal.

Motoring

In a worst-case scenario, could you manage without a car? I decided to try that for six months and to my amazement, six years later, I don't miss it. OK, I live in a city (Bristol), where there is tolerable public transport. Nothing like London, where in many parts of the city there's a bus every thirty seconds, or just about any major city elsewhere in Western Europe; but tolerable. If you too live near public transport, consider this: just having a car sitting outside costs a lot of money even before you turn the key. So, why not try it for a while, and use taxis or rental cars or Car Clubs when needed? You will also get that warm feeling of saving the planet.

And before you say "bus and train fares are very high these days", my question is this: when did you last calculate *all* the costs of running your car, including whatever taxes apply where you live; including insurance, tyres , repairs, as well as fuel, oil, routine servicing, parking etc? And if you are someone who has always traded their car in every two or three years, then depreciation is a major factor.

Even if you don't trade in frequently, depreciation is always a factor. Your car is costing you a lot of money per week just sitting outside your front door, even before you have started the engine. How much is the total over a year? A friend of mine always says that these so-called 'standing costs', including depreciation average £50 ($75) per week. That figure depends of course on how new your car is, how upmarket it is, and how frequently you change it.

That sum could buy a lot of public transport fares and taxis, as well as the occasional hire car for a weekend away. Since I gave up my car, I very rarely take taxis but, when I need to take one, I know that the cost is small, in comparison with what I'm saving – every month – by not running a car. And the loss of flexibility, in being tied to a timetable, is balanced by all the things I can do on a bus or train: people-watch; make phone calls or check e-mails; read (I always have my Kindle with me); snooze; or just watch the world go by. These are hard to do while driving. And if you were about to tell me that you check e-mails while driving, I don't want to know that.

Of course I recognise that if you live in a rural location, or in a town without good public transport, all the above arguments are pretty irrelevant and I hope you've ignored them.

Gas and electricity

These costs have increased greatly in recent times, so shopping around for deals is even more essential. You've probably seen the compare-the-market ads (worth watching just for those wonderful meerkats). You've also seen or heard the ads – or PSAs (public service announcements), as we used to call them back in my days as a hospital radio presenter – about how much you can save by turning your thermostat down just one degree in the winter. However, I'd ignore the ads if you suffer from an arthritic condition or are at risk from a cardiovascular or other significant health viewpoint. In those situations, of course, a comfortable temperature in the home is more important than saving a few pounds.

As many of us know these days, we can often save by buying both gas and electricity from one provider (the so-called 'dual-fuel discount'). Also I'm sure you have been told that energy-efficient bulbs use a fraction of the power and last much longer and that washing clothes at lower temperatures, with modern machines and detergents, is adequate for most purposes. Finally: and you'll have heard this from the green lobby already – don't leave appliances on standby, especially TV, video and digital radio.

Council Tax (Great Britain only)

If you live alone, do you get your single person discount? Also, if you are living on a low income, even if you already get a single person discount, you may be entitled to Council Tax Benefit. This is a means-tested benefit, so be prepared to produce bank statements etc.

Also, could you ask for a review of the Council Tax banding of your home? A word of warning: a review can go in either direction, so do your research first by checking what tax is paid by your neighbours.

Credit card interest

This whole chapter is preaching the message that there is not much point reducing your debts if you start building them up again straight away. Monitor your spending more closely, take advantage of the fact that you get up to six weeks' free credit…but only if you pay off the full balance monthly. Credit card companies will hate you if you always pay the full balance, because they are not making any money from you; but do you care about that?

On the card/cash question: if past experience shows that you are not very self-disciplined, don't be seduced by the convenience of cards. Instead, go back to the cash economy: put all regular financial commitments on Direct Debit, and then generally leave all your cards at home and only draw out as much cash as you've allowed yourself to spend per week. ("There I go again.")

Water rates

Particularly if you live on your own, get a water meter. Then, remember every time you turn on the tap that it's money literally down the drain. For example, a quick shower uses a fraction of the water used by a bath. I'd add "never use a hose in your garden" if you have a water meter, whether or not you've had a hosepipe ban.

Food

In the UK it is widely known how well such budget supermarkets as Lidl and Aldi have done during this recession. The price differences for some items are considerable. Lots of people, who previously would never have gone there, now boast about the great deals they get.

Anyway, for the sake of your health as well as your finances, cut down on convenience foods. You've heard that message, I am sure, from people with far more dietary expertise than yours truly.

Phone/mobile phone/internet connection

There are always good package deals out there and of course the easiest way to compare them is online. But be careful; there are lots of good deals that give you free evening and weekend calls from your landline but, needless to say, if you also sometimes use the phone during the day you could overrun your budget by a substantial margin. Finally, and this will be very controversial for many: do you really need both a mobile phone (cellphone for readers in North America) and a landline? Is that essential to life…or just convenient for your lifestyle? Could you choose one rather than both?

Payment Protection Insurance (PPI)

This form of insurance has had much attention from the UK media for the past few years, after widespread allegations of mis-selling. Many of the allegations have been upheld and providers have been paying out substantial sums as a result of claims.

General insurance (car, property, house contents, etc)

Do you shop around, especially if you are over 50? You don't have to insure your home and contents through your mortgage lender, by the way. Many people seem to think it is compulsory, which is why the lenders can get away with charging high premiums. Sitting in on a money advice session at Citizens Advice, my colleague and I were amazed to find that a client's second-largest item of expenditure was buildings and contents insurance, simply because she – a single mother on low income – believed she was obliged to insure with the mortgage provider. It wasn't true; but that's what they'd told her and, sadly, she believed it. As a result, she was being ripped off.

Some insurances are of course necessary because of the size of the risk and/or because it's a legal requirement, e.g. third party insurance for your car, buildings insurance for your home. For all other insurance, you need to (a) shop around and then (b) ask yourself if it's worth having. Many people these days are taking the 'self-insurance' attitude, especially if the excess is large and/or the size of claim, in the case of home contents cover, is capped, so you lose out both at the top and bottom. A friend told me that she'd never claimed on her contents insurance in thirty years; she calculated the premiums she'd paid over that period could have re-furnished her house several times over.

Teas and coffees out

The coffee-shop culture that's spread across large parts of the world is wonderful but expensive. Could you cut down? If you do, there is no need to overdo the hair-shirt: if you are a real coffee fan, as I am, then you can drink the very best quality at home every day, for a fraction of the cost, keeping coffee-shop visits as a reward 'for good behaviour'.

One of my brothers lives in Canada; he sent me a spoof newspaper report about a man who'd been arrested by the city police and charged with being on a public street *without being in possession of both a takeaway coffee and a mobile phone*. I loved it. That man surely deserved the full force of the law for such bizarre behaviour.

Pub nights

Could you cut your expenditure on drinks by 50%? Your health will benefit as well as your pocket. You may reply that people who are short of money need a drink or three to forget their worries; understandable, but is it getting you where you want to be?

Clothes

Do you need new clothes or do you just fancy them? If you need them, shop around! There are now so many outlets that sell branded items at much-discounted prices – or search the vintage shops or charity shops. Many people, notably one of my daughters, take a pride in always dressing stylishly with clothes bought from charity shops.

Books, CDs, videos, DVDs etc

Do you use the library? Do you even know where it is?

Miscellaneous purchases

Do you look in 'Pound Shops' or charity shops (called 'op-shops' in some countries)? Or are you (like me until I hit my financial 'wall') unaware of where they are? My daughters and I have had a pact for several Christmases; we agreed to a gift limit of £5 ($7.50) per person. It not only saves us all money but is also a lot of fun, as we give more thought to it, rather than throwing money at the task at the last minute.

That reminds me: on the subject of Christmas presents, a few years ago I saw a great TV programme hosted by the American financial guru Alvin Hall; he was interviewing a British couple who had got into serious debt. They had a combined income of about £60 – 70,000 ($90 – 105,000), if I recall. One of the contributory causes seemed to be the spending of vast amounts on expensive Christmas and birthday presents: not just for immediate family and friends, but for extended family, neighbours, acquaintances, etc.

Alvin tried a sneaky (but effective) trick. First he interviewed the couple's sons (in their twenties, I think) and asked what they liked best about Christmas. "Christmas dinner; going to the midnight carol service; etc, etc," came the answers. "What about the presents?" Hall asked. "Well, yes, they are nice too." Then he asked the friends and neighbours if they could remember what presents they had received. Only a month or two after Christmas, none of them could remember.

Alvin played back the tapes of the interviews to this very generous giver. It wasn't recorded whether any permanent change resulted, however. If you enjoy giving, you enjoy giving, and after all it is supposed to be "more blessed to give than to receive". However, in our culture it sometimes seems we became hooked into spending ever-increasing amounts on buying ever-more-expensive gifts for people who didn't need them and maybe didn't even want them.

In Alvin's case-study above, the children were adults. Of course I realise it's very different if we have small children. In that case, peer pressure is an insidious and powerful factor that is hard to resist, even if our debt problem demands it.

In conclusion, on the subject of gifts and referring back to my list in Chapter 1 ('Causes of debt')…Christmas is not an emergency.

What's your personal RPI?

Every month the latest Retail Prices Index of inflation (RPI) is published here in the UK. I am sure something similar is published where you live. The figure always attracts much media attention: approval or shock. Wage and salary negotiations are, naturally enough, affected by the latest figure. It's especially sensitive information for anyone on a fixed income, e.g. retirees, and anyone with a debt problem.

The matter is considered so important and so controversial that a second version was introduced in the UK: the Consumer Price Index (CPI), which excluded some of the costs in the RPI. As there are now two versions, taking that to its logical conclusion, aren't there really 60 million different RPIs in the UK, as no two people's situations are the same?

My point is this: before you spend too much of your precious energy worrying about whether one of the two 'official' inflation figures has increased, think about this. The inflation rate, whether RPI or CPI, is based on a so-called 'basket of commodities'; that basket is supposed to represent the goods and services that the average person purchases. But you are not average; nobody is average; you have choices. Your personal RPI is different from the official RPI (or CPI); hopefully it is lower, or at least it will be after you have followed some of the ideas in this chapter. The choice is yours.

"Cut your grocery shopping bill in half." – Karyn Fleeting, *Moneywise*

This claim at the top of an article in *Moneywise* (the UK's best-selling personal finance magazine, they tell me), certainly caught my eye. I haven't checked out the "by half" claim yet; but lots of the advice was very sound. It came from their blogger Karyn Fleeting, aka Miss Thrifty (www.miss-thrifty.co.uk). I like her site; and the magazine itself, to which I've been a subscriber for years.

Here are the points I liked best:

- "Shop back to front": When you arrive at the supermarket, ignore the displays of fresh fruit and veg near the entrance; head instead for the freezer section, which is usually deeper into the store. Frozen fruit and veg are much cheaper, for sure; they are often fresher, because of the flash-freezing process; and you are less likely to waste food. So start here, she says, and work backwards through the store. A simple and original idea.
- "Closing time": as you probably know, there are usually bargains to be had just before closing time. Best of all, even 24-hour supermarkets close on Sunday evening. So that's the best time of all to shop for bargains.

On the same topic, a guy I know in Bristol says: "Even Waitrose (the UK's most expensive supermarket) is not expensive… provided you don't decide what to have for dinner until you go in there early in the evening and see what's on offer."

- "Step down; look down": it's obvious that you can save money by stepping down a brand level: from branded products to the supermarket's own-label range, or to their value range. (Even Waitrose has one of those, folks!) And you also probably knew that the cheaper products are lower down on the shelves, i.e. out of your eye-line.
- "Look at the back": the newest, i.e. freshest, products tend to be at the back of a display. That makes sense; they want to move the older stock first.

The general point that 'Miss Thrifty' makes is this: "Supermarkets are designed to encourage you to spend as much as possible. So work out what they want you to do; and do the opposite." I like her thinking.

What time of day do you usually go food-shopping?

Alvin Hall, the personal finance guru whom I've mentioned elsewhere in this book, is almost as well known on this side of the Atlantic as he is in his native USA, because of the excellent TV programmes he's presented. He makes a good point, which comes in the same category as Miss Thrifty's advice above, and which I'd paraphrase as follows:

"If you go food shopping when you are hungry, you are more likely to make 'impulse buys' and therefore to spend more. So do your routine food shopping after lunch, not before."

Finally…

- Analyse your spending for the last month. Ask yourself,

"If I were absolutely broke, which of these expenditures could I live without?"

- The cash economy: use Direct Debits for all regular *and essential* payments, cash for everything else.
- Leave at home, or even cut up, all your cards, except maybe one credit card (the one with the lowest interest rate) for dire emergencies and your debit card for minor emergencies. (Is Christmas an emergency? I don't think so. Happens every year.)
- Shop around: utilities (incl. phones), insurance, mortgage, rent etc. Use one of the many online price comparison websites. But you already knew you probably ought to do that.
- Do you really need to run a car?
- Cutting down on meat in your diet *might* improve your health; it will *certainly* save you money.
- Reward yourself (now and then) for outperforming your plan, i.e. when you have a certain amount left at the end of the week, decide to spend *some* of it on a treat.
- Make it a point of honour to put in an hour of 'quality time' with your financial records every week. (That's Alvin Hall's suggestion; and a good one.)

The concept of thrifty living did not come naturally to me. Some of these tips might seem obvious to you; they didn't to me, until my debt crisis came calling. But, as the saying goes, necessity is the mother of invention.

I discovered that I could live very happily on far less money than I had previously thought possible. That I could spend less; and save or invest more. Maybe you will make the same discovery.

"Ordinary riches can be stolen; real riches cannot. In your soul are infinitely precious things that cannot be taken from you." – Oscar Wilde

Resources

Free advice: the charity sector

There are many professionals who can help you for free. First up is your local debt advice office: in my case it was the local bureau of the national charity Citizens Advice ('the CAB' as the local offices are known in the UK). They, and similar organisations, provide support on debt problems free of charge. The CABs employ hundreds of money advisers across the UK and I found them extremely knowledgeable and dedicated people. A word of warning, though: free services of this kind are often overstretched and will continue to be so in the current economic climate. It might take you some time to get an appointment, so contact them without delay.

My local office was helpful in three ways: (a) as a sounding board; (b) as an adviser (after all, they have been dealing with cases like yours and mine for years, so they know what is and is not possible) and (c) they can write letters on your behalf if you want them to.

This third point is valuable in two ways: firstly, it adds credibility to what you say; secondly, it can increase your chances of a successful negotiation. That's because of the principle of 'negotiating with limited authority', i.e. that you can often do better deals if you negotiate through a third party. That creates distance between you and your creditor. I refer elsewhere to this principle of 'negotiating with limited authority'.

So, I was helped first by Citizens Advice and then later by an insolvency practitioner; all free of charge. I hope that the contact details below will help you find suitable and expert support where you live.

Insolvency practitioners

If Plan B is worth investigating further for your situation, then you will need the specialist knowledge of an insolvency practitioner. If this is you, be sure to read Chapter 9.

Contact Details

UK based charities offering personal finance education and/or free debt advice nationwide

Citizens Advice
- Free advice provider; registered charity. Funders include central and local government, charitable trusts, companies and individuals.
- Face-to-face interviews and telephone advice available at local Citizens Advice Bureaux (CABs). Find your nearest bureau in the phone directory, or search at www.citizensadvice.org.uk
- E-mail advice also available at some CABs.
- Advice line: 0844 499 4718
- Online help also available: www.adviceguide.org.uk

The Money Charity (formerly Credit Action)
- Money education charity.
- Spendometer App; Online Budget Builder; The Money Manual; Student Moneymanual; and other resources.
- http://themoneycharity.org.uk/resources/

National Debtline
- Free advice provider; registered charity. Part of the Money Advice Trust, (see below) funded by a mix of private sector donations and Government grants.
- Free factsheets: phone order line.
- Provider of the impressive "CASHflow" system, which helps you work out a budget, draw up a debt manage-

ment plan and send proposals to creditors: http://bit.
ly/1qXYQUi
- 0808 808 4000
- "10 ways to clear your debt", setting out and comparing
your options: http://bit.ly/1oOg4P6
- www.nationaldebtline.org

Business Debtline

The equivalent of National Debtline for self-employed people.
- www.bdl.org.uk
- 0800 197 6026

StepChange (formerly Consumer Credit Counselling Service)

- Free advice provider.
- Registered charity.
- "Works with over 670 partners from large financial
institutions and retailers through to local authorities and
charities."
- Telephone counselling 0800 138 1111 (Freephone in-
cluding all mobiles).
- Online help: http://www.stepchange.org/

The descriptions of the above national organisations are taken
from their websites. Every effort has been taken to ensure the
accuracy of the information presented, which is offered for
information and does not constitute a recommendation.

Local independent debt advice organisations also exist in
many areas and are too numerous to list. But see 'Advice UK'
in the list below, to find one near you.

Other UK-based organisations with helplines or websites on debt and related issues

Disclaimers

- Sorry if this list is UK-centric, because that's where I live.

- Where legal matters are concerned, this book refers to the laws of England and Wales.
- These web links have been checked at the time of going to press. However, no guarantee can be given as to the helplines: many organisations, whether public-sector or charities, are moving more towards online help.

Advice UK (to find a local money advice centre)
020 7407 4070
www.adviceuk.org.uk

Age Concern
0800 00 99 66
www.ageconcern.org.uk

Association of British Credit Unions
0161 832 3694
www.abcul.org/home
…and to find your nearest Credit Union:
www.findyourcreditunion.co.uk/home

BBC Money Box
www.bbc.co.uk/moneybox

Child Benefit Enquiry Line
0845 302 1444
www.hmrc.gov.uk/childbenefit/

Child Support Agency (child maintenance & enforcement commission)
0845 7133 133
www.csa.gov.uk

Cruse (advice & support for people dealing with bereavement)
0844 477 9400
www.crusebereavementcare.org.uk

Debtors Anonymous (worldwide community with telephone & online meetings)

www.debtorsanonymous.org/
…and to find contact details for local meetings in UK:
www.debtorsanonymous.org.uk/
…and for a list of meetings:
http://debtorsanonymous.org.uk/meetings-list

Directgov (the official UK government website for citizens)

www.direct.gov.uk
…and for their debt resources:
www.gov.uk/browse/tax/court-claims-debt-bankruptcy

Energy Ombudsman (disputes with fuel suppliers)

0845 055 0760
www.energy-ombudsman.org.uk

Financial Conduct Authority (the official regulator; provides information for consumers)

Consumer helpline 0800 111 6768
www.fca.org.uk

Financial Ombudsman (complaints about banks, building societies, insurance, pensions etc)

0845 080 1800
www.financial-ombudsman.org.uk

Gamanon (for people and their families affected by gambling addiction)

www.gamanon.org.uk/meetings.php

Gamblers Anonymous (purpose as for Gamanon)

www.gamblersanonymous.org/ga/

Gingerbread (national network for one-parent families)
0800 018 4318
www.gingerbread.org.uk

Help the Aged (now Age UK)
0808 800 6565
www.helptheaged.org.uk

Mind (charity & helpline that helps with mental health problems)
0845 7660 163
www.mind.org.uk

Money Advice Trust, (MAT) (charity formed to develop availability of free, independent debt advice; funded by a mix of private sector donations and Government grants. National Debtline is part of MAT.)
0808 808 4000
www.moneyadvicetrust.org/
…and to download a free .pdf of their booklet 'Dealing With Your Debts', go to http://bit.ly/1m69LuZ

MoneySavingExpert (financial advice site with debt discussion board)
http://forums.moneysavingexpert.com/forumdisplay.php?f=76

Motley Fool (financial advice site)
www.fool.co.uk or www.fool.com

MSN Money (e.g. credit repair, 5 steps)
http://money.uk.msn.com/

National Domestic Violence Helpline
0808 200 0247
www.refuge.org.uk

National Drugs Helpline

0800 77 66 00

www.talktofrank.com

Payplan (commercial debt advice and debt management company)

0800 280 2816

www.payplan.com

Pensions Service

www.thepensionservice.gov.uk

Relate (relationship counselling)

0300 100 1234

www.relate.org.uk

Rights of Women (legal advice helpline for women in England & Wales)

020 7251 6577/8887

www.rightsofwomen.org.uk

Samaritans (confidential emotional support)

0845 790 9090

www.samaritans.org

Saneline (support for mental illness)

0845 767 8000

www.sane.org.uk

Shelter (free housing advice helpline)

0808 800 4444

www.shelter.org.uk

Taxaid (advice about tax problems)

0845 120 3779

www.taxaid.org.uk

Tax Credits Helpline

0845 300 3900
www.hmrc.gov.uk

The Insolvency Service (official advice on bankruptcy & related instruments)

0845 602 9848
www.insolvency.gov.uk

The UK Insolvency Helpline (consumer & business debt advice service)

0800 074 6918
www.insolvencyhelpline.co.uk

Unbiased.co.uk (to find a local IFA (Independent Financial Adviser), mortgage adviser, solicitor or accountant)

0800-085-3250
www.unbiased.co.uk

Note

One sometimes reads criticisms of the helplines of Government departments; but I have found the telephone help given by the UK Insolvency Service and the Pensions Service most helpful and informative.

US financial advice websites: a selection

Retirement

www.BenefitsCheckUp.org, from the National Council on Ageing. Provides information on more than 1,550 public and private benefits programs for seniors in every state and the District of Columbia. Lets seniors or their caregivers enroll directly in such programs, based on eligibility. And if you know someone who needs help, you can arrange to have BenefitsCheckUp send that person information.

Has application forms for more than 250 programs that pay for drug prescriptions and other health care costs.

www.ChooseToSave.org, a site developed by the Employee Benefit Research Institute to promote savings. Has an interactive tool – BallPark Estimate – to help calculate how much you need to save for retirement. Also lists dozens of calculators to help you save, invest and budget.

www.AARP.org, a leading source of information for those 50 and older. It covers topics such as debt, savings and Social Security. AARP also teams with financial firms on co-branded auto insurance and health and life insurance, often at a discount. (It receives revenue from these firms when consumers sign up for AARP financial products.)

Banking and credit cards

www.Bankrate.com provides information on everything from checking and savings accounts to mortgages and credit cards. Voluminous data, presented clearly and concisely. Bankrate surveys 4,800 financial institutions to find the highest yields – in your state and nationally – on CDs, checking and savings accounts. You can hunt for the lowest rates on mortgages and student loans. Calculators can help you see whether you're on track to finance a college education, retire in 10 years or pay off your debt. (USA TODAY, through a partnership with Bankrate, posts some of these calculators on USATODAY.com.) In addition, Bankrate gives tips on improving a credit score, budgeting and home buying.

www.CardRatings.com provides objective credit card rating information, with about 1,100 card descriptions, plus 19,000 reviews by consumers of nearly 1,000 cards. Highly rated cards are recognized with a "Top Rated Card" award seal.

www.CardWeb.com supplies information on credit and other cards, such as prepaid cards, ATM cards and phone cards, along with industry news. Includes lists of low-rate and no-annual-fee cards. Among the calculators on the site, one can help you determine how long it will take to pay off card debt.

(Acknowledgements for the above to *USA TODAY.*)

Finally, www.fool.com : The Motley Fool; one of the best-known financial info sites both on your side of the Atlantic and mine.

Further reading

Books
- *Eliminate Your Debt Like a Pro* – Steve Rhode
- *Get out of debt with Alvin Hall* – Alvin Hall
- *Get out of debt forever* – Lorraine Turner
- *Getting out of debt & staying out* – Tony Palmer
- *The Debt Doctor* – Robert Leach
- *Detox your finances…for women* – Justine Trueman
- *How to Get Out of Debt, Stay Out of Debt & Live Prosperously* – Jerrold Mundis
- *Fear & Loathing in my bank account* – Sean Coghlan
- *Win-win negotiating: turning conflict into agreement* – Fred E Jandt
- *Smart saving tips* – Jane Furnival

Sample letters

This is just a selection of 'sample letters' for a variety of circumstances. Some of them are very similar to sample letters that a debt advice organisation would provide; and some were in fact written in consultation with my adviser at the local CAB. Some were written later, in response to situations that happened during my progress towards a 'Plan C' type solution.

No two debt situations are identical, so it may well be

that none of these exactly fits your situation. However, I trust that they will give you some ideas and that you can adapt the appropriate paragraphs.

Naturally you will have to add the key facts e.g. creditor's name and address, the name of the contact person at the creditor organisation if you know it, your own name & address and finally account number(s).

I'm planning to put versions of these letters on my website (www.michaelmacmahon.com), from whence you will be able to copy and edit them for your own purposes.

Note

None of these letters is for use in a 'Plan B'-type solution, as the correspondence with creditors and/or intermediaries would in such a case be conducted on your behalf by your Trustee or Insolvency Practitioner.

1   Holding letter with token offer, plus request to freeze interest and charges.
2   Response to letter ignoring request to freeze interest and charges.
3   Response to letter ignoring previous letter(s).
4   Stating intention to pay in full and asking for time.
5   Offer of self-managed instalment-based pro rata settlement.
6   Offer for "full and final settlement" with third-party funding.
7   Offer for "full and final settlement" but funded by pension lump-sum or drawdown.
8   Offer acceptance form (to be sent with letters of types 5, 6 or 7).
9   Response to acceptance of full and final offer; payment pending other acceptances.
10   Response to rejection of instalment offer.
11   Response to rejection of "full and final settlement" offer.
12   Response to a counter-offer.

13 Response to an intermediary chasing you on behalf of a creditor.
14 Response to an intermediary unaware of your previous offer.
15 Letter to utility provider or other trade creditor re arrears.

All letters need, of course, to contain the following basic information:

Your address
Name of Creditor
Address of Creditor
For the attention of [if you have a named contact]
Date
Re: Account no. xxxxxx

Dear Sirs [or "Dear Mr X" or "Dear Ms X" if you have a named contact]

[text]

Yours faithfully [or "yours sincerely" or "regards" if you are communicating with a named contact]

[signature]
Type, or write clearly, your name under your signature

1. Holding letter with a token offer

I am having difficulties with my finances at present because of [state the reason for your difficulties briefly] and I have sought the help of [state name of the advice organisation whose help you have sought, even if you haven't yet had your first session]. With their help I shall be completing a standard financial statement.

In the meantime I have very little discretionary income/no

discretionary income. [Delete as appropriate.]

I am currently job-hunting [if appropriate] and in receipt of Jobseekers' Allowance. [If appropriate.]

As a matter of urgency I am working with my advisers to find a solution. As a token of goodwill, I propose in the short term to pay £1 per month to each of my creditors and I hope that this is acceptable to you. My cheque is enclosed.

I also enclose a list of my creditors. [If your advisers agree to this line.]

I respectfully request that for the time being you suspend recovery action on this account and prevent further interest or charges from accruing, so as not to exacerbate the overall debt situation.

I shall be in touch again soon with a specific offer.

2. Response to letter ignoring request to freeze interest and charges

Thank you for your letter/telephone message of [insert date of their letter or message].

In my letter of [insert date of your letter] I informed you that I was working with [name of advice organisation] to resolve my debt situation and I requested a moratorium on interest and charges for the time being, until I can come up with a proposal.

So far I have not had a response to this request. I would thus be grateful to receive your confirmation that this is acceptable to you.

3. Response to letter that ignores your previous letter(s)

I have received your letter of [insert date] regarding the above account. Unfortunately it does not refer to the proposal I have made in my letter of [insert date].

I can only assume that the letters must have crossed and so I am enclosing a copy of my last letter. I look forward to your favourable response.

4. Stating your intention to pay in full but requesting time

I am having difficulties with my finances at present because of…and I have sought the help of [state name of organisation whose help you have sought, even if you haven't yet had your first session]. With their help I shall be completing a standard financial statement.

I intend to satisfy this debt in full but I shall need some time to do so. As a matter of urgency I am working with my advisers so as to work out a payment schedule.

As a token of goodwill, I propose in the short term to pay £1 per month to each of my creditors and I hope that this is acceptable to you. My cheque is enclosed/I have set up a Standing Order [delete as appropriate].

I respectfully request that for the time being you suspend recovery action on this account and prevent further interest or charges from accruing, so as not to exacerbate the overall debt situation. Please also confirm that this is acceptable to you.

I shall be in touch again soon with a specific offer. Meanwhile I would appreciate receiving your confirmation that you are able to accept the temporary proposals stated above.

5. Offer of self-managed instalment-based pro rata settlement (non-priority debts)

Further to previous correspondence, I now wish to make an offer to settle the above debt.

I enclose a copy of my financial statement from which you will see that I have very little discretionary income. As a result I am making pro rata offers to all my creditors and I am able to offer you £xxx per month. I propose to make the first payment on xx.xx.xx.

I look forward to your agreement to this proposal. In the meantime please also confirm that you will suspend interest and other charges on my account for as long as regular payments are made.

6. Offer for "full and final settlement", with lump sum provided by third-party funding (non-priority debts)

Further to previous correspondence and my interim payment of £1/month, I have been in consultation with my advisers and I now have an opportunity to make you a proposal.

I now have some funds on offer from third parties in order to settle my debts and I wish to do so on a pro rata basis.

The best offer I can make to all my unsecured creditors is xx pence in the £ for full and final settlement. This produces an offer of £xxxx on the above account.

The offer is made on the understanding that, if accepted, neither you nor any intermediary acting on your behalf will take any action to enforce or pursue this debt in any way and that I will be released from any further liability.

This proposal is also contingent on my getting the agreement of all my creditors.

The funds I have on offer are not available indefinitely. Please, therefore, indicate your acceptance of this offer as soon as possible by signing and returning the attached reply sheet.

Enclosure: notice of acceptance

7. Offer for "full and final settlement", funded by pension lump-sum or drawdown (non-priority debts)

Further to previous correspondence and my interim payment of £1/month, I have been in consultation with my advisers and I now have an opportunity to make you a proposal.

I have some personal pension funds and, because of my age, I am able to draw on these funds. I am prepared to do this in order to make offers on a pro rata basis for full and final settlement.

The best offer I can make to all my unsecured creditors is xx pence in the £ for full and final settlement. This produces an offer of £xxxx on the above account.

The offer is made on the understanding that, if accepted, neither you nor any intermediary acting on your behalf will take any action to enforce or pursue this debt in any way and that I will be released from any further liability.

This proposal is also contingent on my getting the agreement of all my creditors.

Please indicate your acceptance of this offer by signing and returning the attached reply sheet.

Enclosure: notice of acceptance

8. "Notice of acceptance" form (to be sent with letters of types 5, 6 or 7)

To: [type your own name/address]

Account no.

Offer: [type in the amount you offer that creditor]

We accept the above offer in full and final settlement of your account with us.

Signed

Name of signatory

For and on behalf of

Date

Payment address, if different from correspondence address:

9. Response to acceptance of full and final offer; payment pending other acceptances

Thank you for confirming your acceptance of my offer for full and final settlement.

So far I have not yet received the agreement of all my creditors to my offer. I am not, therefore, yet in a position to release the funds offered, as my advisers inform me that the pro rata offer must be accepted by all creditors or my debt management plan might not stand.

In the interim I am enclosing, as requested (if appropriate) a further cheque for £1 as a token of intent. I request your patience and you can be assured of my best efforts to conclude the matter to everyone's satisfaction.

10. Response to rejection of instalment offer

Thank you for your letter/phone message of [date] rejecting my offer.

I have a problem in responding in that I have made the same pro rata offer to all my creditors. I have received acceptances from several of them.

My advisers at [name of advice organisation] have cautioned me that I cannot treat any creditor preferentially. May I thus ask you to reconsider my offer?

11. Response to rejection of "full & final settlement" offer

I refer to recent correspondence regarding your account and your rejection of my offer for full and final settlement.

I can now inform you that several of my creditors [name them if you have significant acceptances] have accepted my offer on the same basis as made to you. I am therefore drawing down the funds I need to make the settlement.

I am being advised by [name of your advisers]. The net effect of the advice I have received is that I cannot offer any of my creditors a higher dividend than any of the others. The offer must be pro rata and that was the basis of my offer. Therefore I am not permitted to improve on the offer for any individual creditor, whatever the circumstances.

In view of the above, I ask you to reconsider your offer and get back to me.

12. Response to a counter-offer

Thank you for your letter of [insert date] in response to mine of [insert date]. While your proposal is reasonable, I am afraid that in the short term it is not possible for me to comply with it.

As you will see from the enclosed list, I have [insert number of] creditors. As you will also see from the enclosed financial statement/statement of affairs, I have very little disposable income/ no disposable income. [delete as appropriate] I would be happy to pay your company more if I could, but I am sure you will realise I am unable to do so and in fact am not permitted to do so now that my affairs are under scrutiny.

I therefore hope that you can accept my offer.

13. Response to an intermediary chasing you on behalf of a creditor

Intermediary's account no.
Name of creditor
Creditor's account no. [If different.]

Further to recent correspondence, whilst I respect your position and that of your principal, my situation is that I have made the same offer to all my unsecured creditors.

I have been told by my advisers at [insert name of advice organisation] that I should not treat any creditor preferentially. For this reason I cannot improve my offer. May I therefore ask you to request your client to reconsider?

I hope to receive a favourable reply from you.

14. To intermediary unaware of any type of offer

Intermediary's account number
Name of creditor
Creditor's account no. [If different.]

I refer to your recent letter/phone message, [delete as appropriate] from which I understood that you were not aware I had made an offer to your client.

For the sake of good order, therefore, I enclose a copy of that offer.

I have been advised that it is necessary to make an equivalent offer to all my unsecured creditors on a pro-rata basis. This is what I have done. I therefore urge you to use your influence with your client to secure acceptance of my offer.

15. To utility provider or other trade creditor re arrears

Owing to financial problems I am currently experiencing, I would like to request a delay in the settlement of my account.

I would be grateful if I could postpone payment for xx months and look forward to your confirmation that this is acceptable.

Sources of other sample letters: for UK readers

There are also sample letters in the information pack entitled 'Dealing with Your Debt', available from all Citizens Advice Bureaux.

Most useful of all is a tool for generating sample letters on National Debtline's website: all you have to do is select the type of letter, insert your own details, adjust to your own circumstances and, hey presto, you have a letter.

Budgeting tools & resources

CASHflow

National Debtline, mentioned elsewhere, have developed this very useful system. It can help you budget, manage your debt and prepare proposals to creditors. It's set out in a format that many creditors and advice agencies use.

You can access the tool online at http://bit.ly/1qXYQUi or get a paper copy by phoning them at 0808 808 4000.

Money Saving Expert

If you're reading this in the United Kingdom, you are probably aware of Martin Lewis's 'Money Saving Expert' site. If not, find it! They have a whole section on budgeting, which is well worth a look: http://www.moneysavingexpert.com/banking/Budget-planning.

Smartphone apps

There are many apps for smartphones, which will simply help you track how you spend your money. That increased awareness of how much you spend, and on what, will probably cause you to reduce your expenditure within a very short time.

The apps will work on tablets too, of course, but it's probably best to use your smartphone for this purpose because, like 99% of the population, you probably have the thing with you when you've just spent the money. That's the time to record the information: don't reply on your memory to do it later.

My mentioning an app here does not constitute a recommendation, because I am definitely no expert on the subject. For a start, at my relatively advanced age there is a limit to how much 'small print' I want to read on a smartphone screen. (At least I've got one of the things, which I hope will impress you.)

So I asked one of my daughters. She uses an app called Pocket Expense and speaks highly of it.

Here's an independent review. At least I'm guessing it's independent, as the site reviews so much software. http://financialsoft. about.com/od/pdasoftware/ss/5-Best-Ipad-Personal-Finance-Apps-For-2013_5.htm.

Note

Although this review says 'Pocket Expense for iPad' – and thus for iPhone too – there is also an Android version.

Do your own Google search and I am sure you will find many others. The wonderful world of apps is expanding fast, thus I am sure twenty more budgeting apps will have hit the market since this book went to press.

'The Spendometer'

I've mentioned this elsewhere and it was the first piece of personal expense tracking software of which I became aware. It was developed by, or for, Credit Action, now called The Money Charity – a major non-profit organisation in this field. Although it's been around for a while, so far it is only available for Apple devices, 'due to technical issues', which is a pity. www.spendometer.co.uk.

Discretionary income table

In Chapter 7, I discussed disposable and discretionary income. Here's a template for calculating your own discretionary income. I suggest that you include only essentials in the boxes for costs.

Then you might wish to use the right-hand column in the expenditure section, to conduct an exercise called 'if push came to shove'. In other words: what is your 'survival budget'?

How much could you trim those 'essential costs', if everything depended on it?

When I went through my own debt crisis, I found that I could manage without many things I had always thought were essential.

	Income		
A	**Total income** (either from wage, salary or self-employed income and/or pensions, benefits or investments)		
B	Income tax (if not already deducted)		
C	Net income after direct tax [= A minus B]		
D	National Insurance (UK) (or payroll tax wherever you live)		
E	Local taxes, e.g. Council Tax in Great Britain		
F	**'Disposable' income** [= C minus D & E]		
	Essential expenditure	Current	"Survival budget"
G	Mortgage or rent		
H	Essential utilities (water, gas, electricity)		
I	Food essentials		
J	Transport to & from work (include car standing costs *only* if car essential for work)		
K	Other essentials (e.g. home insurance)		
L	Prior commitments (e.g. loan or card repayments) but only if non-negotiable		
M	**Total essential living costs** [add G to L inclusive]		
N	**'Discretionary' income** (per week/fortnight/month*) [= F minus M]		

Your discretionary income is just that; it is 'at your discretion'. That means you can use it EITHER for discretionary (i.e. non-essential) expenditure, OR to pay down debt.

It's your decision!

Note

If most of your income is received monthly, then I suggest that you insert all the figures on a 'per calendar month' basis. Similarly, express them weekly if that's how most of your income is received. However, if you live in rented accommodation and pay rent fortnightly, as is often the case, you might prefer to do everything on a fortnightly basis. Some benefits and pensions, on the other hand, are paid every four weeks (i.e. 'per lunar month'; don't ask the logic of the people who thought up that system). The important thing is to be consistent.

Discretionary/disposable income: online calculation tools

(Open the files and then choose the one that suits you best.)

www.britishinvasion.co.uk/soa/soaedit.php. (Source: The Motley Fool website. This is a statement of affairs calculator but it includes all expenses.)

www.moneyadviceservice.org.uk/yourmoney/interactive/budget_planner.aspx (to access the UK Government's Money Advice Service budget planner).

What's Next?

I hope that you have found this book useful. If it has shown you that there is a solution out there to the debt problem you are facing, and if it has given you some ideas about how to seek that solution, it has fulfilled its purpose.

I blog from time to time on issues of personal finance. If you have questions, or if you'd simply like to keep in touch with me and with other readers of this book, you can do so via my website: www.michaelmacmahon.com.

I'll be glad to hear from you.

Finance Coaching

At various points in this book I have said, "if you had a coach or counsellor, they might ask you…" or similar.

If you think you might benefit from talking to such a person, then you can either:

- Get in touch with me, as I'm a coach, or
- Check out the Coach Directory of The Coaching Academy. They are the world's largest trainer of coaches (they trained me). Their directory is a valuable resource: http://www.coach-search.co.uk/index.asp.

Michael J MacMahon, Bristol, UK

About the Author

Michael J MacMahon is an author, a coach and a speaker. He's also a voice actor. He was born in 1943 in Haverfordwest, Pembrokeshire. Michael was educated at St George's College, Weybridge and Imperial College, London. He now lives in Bristol in the West of England.

During a career in the chemical industry, including British Oxygen and Unilever, he became Managing Director of a UK subsidiary of Holmen – a major Swedish-owned multinational group manufacturing pulp, paper and chemicals. He then set up and ran a training consultancy for seven years with blue-chip clients in Scandinavia.

He was a fundraiser and a media spokesman for The Stroke Association – a major UK charity in the medical sector. When he reached the magic age of 65 he decided not to retire, choosing reinvention instead.

Finally...

"Do not value money for any more nor any less than its worth; it is a good servant but a bad master." – Alexandre Dumas

CPSIA information can be obtained at www.ICGtesting.com
Printed in the USA
LVOW11s1910240315

431820LV00005B/634/P